CONTENTS

A GUIDE TO EFFECTIVE
SERMON DELIVERY

THE MOMENT OF
TRUTH

WAYNE V. MCDILL

BROADMAN
& HOLMAN
PUBLISHERS

Nashville, Tennessee

© 1999
by Wayne McDill
All rights reserved

Ten-Digit ISBN: 0–8054–1827–X
Thirteen-Digit ISBN: 978–0–8054–1827–9

Published by Broadman & Holman Publishers, Nashville, Tennessee
Editorial Team: Leonard G. Goss, John Landers, Sandra Bryer
Page Design and Typesetting: TF Designs, Mt. Juliet, Tennessee

Dewey Decimal Classification: 251
Subject Heading: PREACHING/SERMON DELIVERY
Library of Congress Card Catalog Number: 98-12003

Scripture quotations are from
the New King James Version, copyright © 1979, 1980, 1982,
Thomas Nelson, Inc.

Some images copyright www.artoday.com

Library of Congress Cataloging-in-Publication Data

McDill, Wayne V.
The moment of truth : a guide to effective sermon delivery / by
    Wayne V. McDill
        p. cm.
Includes bibliographical references and index.
    ISBN 0-8054-1827-X (pbk.)
    1. Preaching. I. Title.
BV4211.2.M175   1999
251 --- dc21
                                                                92-12003
                                                                      CIP
        12 13 14 15 16 17 18 19 20 15 14 13 12 11 10 09 08 07 06 05

THE MOMENT OF
TRUTH

THE MOMENT OF TRUTH

T he moment of truth. What does this mean? We are dealing of course, with sermon delivery. But we must not think of it as the mere presentation of a persuasive speech on a religious theme. Preaching is much more than that. God has ordained to use man as His agent of revelation. He has sent His agent forth to preach. This is His method. It is His way of keeping the original vision alive. It is His method of teaching and renewing His people. It is His method of communicating the good news of salvation in Jesus Christ. On every occasion preaching has this potential. It is the *moment of truth.*

"Moment" means, in the first place, an indeterminate but brief period of time. A moment can be but a few seconds, or it can conceivably cover hours. We can say, "One moment, please" to ask for a very brief pause. Or, we can say of longer periods, "It was a moment to remember." As to sermon delivery, it is an event in time. Oral communication unfolds in time. The sermon is a presentation in time of a sequence of thoughts centered in a single biblical idea.

A sermon idea is not a sermon. A sermon outline is not a sermon. A sermon manuscript is not a sermon. A sermon only comes into existence in the *moment*, in the preaching. However thorough the preparation, both of message and messenger, they are but the anticipation of a sermon. When we read Whitefield's sermons, they do not impress us now as they did those who heard him preach. We can almost hear them say, "You would just have to be there." It is obvious that these tran-

1

scripts are not the sermons. They are like a corpse lying in repose. Only the form remains; the life and breath are gone.

The *moment of truth* is that occasion when the sermon lives. It comes forth from the mouth of the preacher and takes shape in the mind of the hearer. The dynamism of dialog is present. The audience reads the preacher—his tone of voice, his facial expressions, his movements, his energy and animation—and every signal blends with his words to create a message. And the preacher reads his audience, scanning faces for silent comments, body language for unspoken attitudes, listening to the subtle message of verbal response.

When nothing is left but the words, lifeless on the page, the sermon is gone. Only a report of it remains. Only the memory of the *moment* continues in the minds of preacher and hearers alike.

It is not just any moment, however, it is the moment of *truth*. It is the breaking upon the minds of the hearers of the very truth of God. In this truth they hear the "great alternative," ideas that would never arise in the carnal mind, ideas that provide an option for faith that can only come by the revelation of God. And this is the moment, the moment of revelation, the moment in which God speaks. None can experience this hearing of the voice of God and ever be the same again.

Here the old, old Story is retold and God speaks through it again to give meaning for the hearer in his own experience. The old story completes the hearer's story, giving his story a new beginning as to where he came from, and a new ending as to where he is going. As the truth of God breaks in upon his thinking, everything is open to question. He came to this moment with his mind made up. All the pieces were there, though some broken and frayed with the pain of life. But now he has heard the Story. Now a new light has shown upon his life. This is the moment of truth.

On any given Sunday those who come to worship are searching for answers. More than half of them are hurting. Some grieve over losses they were not prepared to make. Others worry about the possibility of trouble that looms on the horizon. Some are weary with life, unsure where to turn, fearful of making yet more mistakes and reaping their consequences. So they come to hear. They lift their weary and hopeful faces to a messenger who is called to speak for God. Will he offer any hope? Will he give reason for faith? This is the moment of truth.

The preacher experiences the moment of truth as a crisis of faith and revelation for himself as well. He believes he is God's messenger. He is under a divine mandate to proclaim the very Word of God from Scripture. "Who is sufficient for these things?" he cries with Paul. And the answer is clear. No one. But he stands to preach anyway. He has prepared as best he can. He has prayed. His hands are sweaty, his thoughts swirl, his feet restless, his throat dry. But he is determined to be a faithful messenger of God. It is the moment of truth.

It is not the preparation that is the moment. He may have been inspired to a degree in the study. These ideas from Scripture do set our hearts ablaze. But those hours in the study are nothing like this, this *moment*. He has prayed, but he is not confident that his prayers were sufficient. He prays again as he looks out over the faces of the people. "What do they need, Lord? How shall I feed Your lambs? Unless You speak, my words will be as a sounding brass or clanging cymbal. Speak to Your people. Only You know their hearts. Give them Your word." It is the moment of truth.

The word "moment" also means "of special significance or importance." The moment of truth in preaching carries the promise of divine presence and blessing, of life-changing grace for every need. Of all the moments of the week, this one trembles with potential and expectancy. What can be more *momentous* than to meet God, to hear His voice, to sense His presence, to know His will. What can be more *momentous* than to respond in faith to His call, to conduct eternally significant business, to have one's whole outlook changed in the span of a moment. There is no time like this moment of truth.

The preaching hour is momentous because the Spirit of God comes to empower the word for preacher and hearer alike. He edits the sermon as it unfolds from the preacher's mind. He enlivens the thoughts and testifies to their truth. Like flames of fire touching every listener, the Spirit warms their hearts and awakens their understanding. He convicts the unbeliever of sin and righteousness and judgment. He lifts up Jesus and draws men to Him. He encourages the hopeless and comforts the grieving. Like a heavenly breeze, He refreshes the people of God. It is the moment of truth.

The delivery of a sermon is a momentous occasion for the preacher as well. It is here that he takes on the mantle of his calling as nowhere

3

else. Of all the opportunities for ministry he encounters in his week of work, none has the man-hours of potential of one sermon. It is in this moment that he calls his flock to the original vision of the Christian movement. It is here, at this moment, that he exercises his pastoral leadership most effectively. It is here, in the moment of truth, that he ministers the grace of God in heaping portions. This moment, when the people of God gather around the Word of God with the messenger of God, is the *moment of truth*.

CHAPTER ONE

GOD'S PLAN FOR PREACHING

H omiletics, the art of writing and preaching sermons, is central to any study of preaching. *Hermeneutics*, the interpretation of literature such as the Bible, is also vital for preaching. A third area, *speech communication*, deals with communication as it relates to human speech, including preparing and making public speeches. A study of preaching must also take *theology* into consideration since preaching is essentially the proclamation of a theological message. Basic to preaching is, of course, a study of *biblical literature*, including the content, history, and languages of the Old and New Testaments.

> *"Unless we understand God's purpose for preaching, the rest is more or less irrelevant."*

In the Bible preaching is a key element in the dramatic story of God's revelation. Authentic preaching was not an invention of man to spread his theological ideas. God called chosen ones out of the ordinary business of their lives to proclaim to their neighbors what He wanted them to know. Their preaching was often a life or death matter, for the flood was coming, the enemy armies were marching, the fires of hell were burning. It was vital that man hear from God.

Preaching can be rightly understood only as a function of the revelation of God. The Greek word for "revelation" is *apocalypsis*, meaning "that which is unveiled." God removes the veil of mystery and shows man a glimpse of His majesty and His purpose. He is both the subject (the one revealing) and the object (the one revealed) of revelation. He alone can make Himself and His purpose known.

We may study the presentation of sermons from the viewpoint of the preacher, or the audience, or the times, or the church, or moral values, or any number of other perspectives. Though each of these vantage points is important, the most basic consideration is the purpose of God for preaching. Unless we understand that, the rest is more or less irrelevant. This chapter examines some of the theological themes that help to form a biblical understanding of the place of preaching in God's purpose. After a survey of these themes we will construct a theological definition of preaching that takes these factors into account.

THE GOD WHO SPEAKS

In his discussion of the theology of preaching, Fred Craddock begins with the silence of God.[1] In the noisy, murmuring world of today, in which everyone talks incessantly about everything, he says, the preacher does well to remember that it was out of the silence that God spoke. Out of the quiet stillness of eternity, God's voice broke upon the uncreated nothingness. "Let there be light," He said, and there was light (Gen 1.3). When He needn't say a word, He spoke out of the ageless silence, and in His self-revelation ultimately reached out to man.

If God had not chosen to reveal Himself, He would remain fully hidden to man. Isaiah spoke of God as the One who "hides" Himself (45.15). "No one has seen God at any time," wrote John. "The only begotten Son . . . has declared Him" (John 1.18). Paul described Him as "dwelling in unapproachable light, whom no man has seen or can see" (1 Tim 6.16). "How unsearchable are His judgments," he writes, "and His ways past finding out" (Rom 11.33). Though man has searched everywhere and guessed what might be beyond his search, it is only by revelation that he can know anything of God.

Al Mohler puts it simply: "True preaching begins with this confession: we preach because God has spoken."[2] The Bible reveals God as sovereign, all powerful, all knowing, omnipresent, loving, merciful, and gracious. No less significant an attribute of God than these is that He is *self-revealing*. He is the God who speaks. The Creator who spoke the worlds

> *"When He needn't say a word, He spoke out of the ageless silence."*

6

into being revealed Himself through nature, where "His invisible attributes are clearly seen, being understood by the things that are made, even His eternal power and Godhead . . ." (Rom 1.20). But this *general* revelation was not the full extent of God's self-revelation.

God also made Himself known in a more direct way. He spoke to men and through men to reveal His nature and purpose in more specific terms. From his first instructions to Adam, throughout the Old and New Testaments, to His cryptic communication to John on the Isle of Patmos, God has spoken. This *special* revelation had its climax in the person of Jesus Christ. "God, who at various times and in various ways spoke in time past to the fathers by the prophets, has in these last days spoken to us by His Son" (Heb 1.1, 2).

Not only was God revealing Himself in personal incarnational terms in Jesus of Nazareth, the words of Jesus were the very words of God. Jesus said, "If you had known Me, you would have known My Father also; . . ." (John 14.7). He also said, "and the word which you hear is not Mine but the Father's who sent Me" (John 14.24). Here was the God who speaks declaring His thoughts clearly in the words of Jesus. Here was a voice men could understand, gestures they could see, facial expressions they could watch, a message in their own language, all from the very person of God.

Fred Craddock emphasizes that preaching follows revelation, not only in purpose but also in method. He writes, "At the risk of sounding presumptuous, it can be said that we are learning our method of communication from God. In other words, from the transaction we call revelation we understand and implement the transaction we call preaching. That is, the way of God's Word in the world is the way of the sermon in the world."[3]

Authentic biblical preaching is an extension of the self-revealing activity of God. Just as He has spoken through the ages with the voice of men, He continues to speak today through preaching. Preaching is vital today "because it does what God did in his self-disclosure to Israel, in his revelation to the prophets and apostles, in the fullness of his revelation in Jesus," writes Clyde Fant. "It provides a medium of revelation which enables the eternal Word to maintain its living, dynamic character and encounter our concrete situation."[4]

THE LIVING WORD

Since God is by nature One who speaks, His word becomes a vital factor in our study of preaching. The words *dabar* in the Old Testament and *logos* and *rhema* in the New are the common Hebrew and Greek terms for "word," meaning "a spoken utterance, a saying or speech." John wrote, "In the beginning was the Word, and the Word was with God, and the Word was God" (John 1.1). The "Word" is equated here with God's own being, His person. This is a special use of the word *logos* not employed in the rest of John's Gospel. It emphasizes that self-revelation is so intrinsic to the nature of God that Jesus, the Son, is called "the Word."

In the biblical view, words, once uttered, have a life of their own. This is especially true of blessings or curses, such as the blessing of Jacob which could not be recalled (Gen 27). God's words always have the power necessary to their purpose. Isaiah pictures them doing their assigned work on their own. "So shall My word be that goes forth from My mouth; It shall not return to Me void, But it shall accomplish what I please, And it shall prosper in the thing for which I sent it" (Isa 55.11).

> *"Self-revelation is so intrinsic to the nature of God that Jesus, the Son, is called 'the Word.'"*

It is difficult for us to grasp the significance of "word" for God's revelation. We think of "word" as a unit of language rather than a powerful idea. To understand what "word" of God means in these key passages, it might be helpful to substitute the word "truth." We think of the *truth* of Scripture as powerful and effective for sorting out ideas and attitudes from God's viewpoint. It is the *truth* of God that is set among His people to guide them, to convict them of sin, to show them who God is and who they are in Christ. This is what the living word is.

This Word of God has a dramatic effect on the hearer. "For the word of God is living and powerful, and sharper than any two-edged sword, piercing even to the division of soul and spirit, and of joints and marrow, and is a discerner of the thoughts and intents of the heart" (Heb 4.12). The Word of God penetrates deep into the heart and mind of the hearer. It separates between the natural man and the spiritual man. It gives a basis for judging not only one's ideas, but also one's motives. When this word is heard, the hearer cannot be unaffected by its power.

Preaching is to proclaim the Word of God. It is obvious, however, that many a sermon is heard without hearing the Word of God. Most sermons are largely the opinions of the preacher. Though the religious views of a godly person might be of some help to a congregation, the real need is for a word from God, the very Word of God. The only way to ensure that the Word of God is heard in the sermon is to allow that Word of God to come through the sermon from the text of Scripture. In a real and actual sense every word of Scripture is the Word of God. To the degree that the biblical text shapes the sermon, to that extent it is possible for the Word of God to be heard in the sermon.

He Who Has Ears to Hear

Who will hear this powerful Word of God? The Bible makes clear that many may be within the sound of that word, but not all will hear. In the dramatic call of Isaiah, we stand in awe of the vision of God and the experience of His prophet. But then we read of His assignment, with its gloomy prediction, "Go, and tell this people: 'Keep on hearing, but do not understand; Keep on seeing, but do not perceive'" (Isa 6.9). The prophet was sent to a people not likely to listen, but he must be faithful to preach nonetheless.

Jesus appealed to His audience to hear His word, "He who has ears to hear, let him hear!" (Matt 11.15). He knew that some of those before Him would not hear. When His disciples asked Him why He taught the people in parables, He explained, "I speak to them in parables, because seeing they do not see, and hearing they do not hear, nor do they understand" (Matt 13.13). The disciples, however, were enabled to hear. Jesus said, "But blessed are your eyes for they see, and your ears for they hear" (Matt 13.16).

"The process of oral communication is challenging enough, even without the spiritual factors that hinder reception of the preached word."

Consider the nature of man as hearer of the Word of God. He is fallen in sin (Rom 3.23), does not understand the things of God (1 Cor 2.14), and is hostile toward God in his mind (Rom 8.7). The preacher is not always addressing a receptive audience, even among Christians, for the carnal Christian cannot receive the Word of God (1 Cor 3.2). The barriers in his nature are multiple. There are ideas and attitudes that form strongholds against the knowledge of God (2 Cor 10.5).

When does one actually "hear" in the biblical sense? The word means more than just receiving the sound waves of a spoken message. "Hear" means to receive the message, understand it, and obey it. But in Jesus' parable, the sower finds only a fourth portion of the seed falling on good soil, for there are the barriers of shallowness, of worldliness, and of the devil's work to remove the word (Matt 13.18-23). Paul writes that in the last days even the believers will turn away (2 Tim 4.3, 4). The process of oral communication is challenging enough, even without the spiritual factors that hinder reception of the preached word.

In spite of these barriers, the preacher is to preach the word faithfully. Though he aims for a response from his audience, he knows that the response will not always be positive. He cannot measure his faithfulness by the response. The danger ever looms over the preacher that he will find himself trying to please them, not by adapting his style to them but by presenting a message more to their liking.

Paul's commitment was to adapt himself so fully to his audience that he might overcome the barriers to their reception of the word. Recognizing the importance of the audience in the communication process, the apostle wrote that he adapted his preaching and his behavior to every audience he faced. He adapted to culture, language, religion, race, social position. His philosophy becomes a key theological principle for every preacher, "I have become all things to all men that I might by all means save some" (1 Cor 9.22).

Audience analysis and adaptation are basic responsibilities of the preacher of the gospel. Realizing the difficulty of getting a hearing for the Word of God, he adjusts his presentation to the audience before him. Not only do spiritual factors affect the communication connection, a number of cultural elements can also get in the way. The worldview, thinking processes, social structures, language, and decision-making processes of a people will determine how they hear the message.[5] Like Paul, the wise preacher will take all this into account to get a hearing.

In a sense, the preacher is himself a hearer. He does not stand aloof from the people as he preaches. He is called from among the people as God's chosen spokesman. Unless he first hears the message for his own life, he will be ill prepared to proclaim it to others. All preaching is interpretation. The preacher's interpretation will naturally arise out of his own experience with God and His Word. He will not likely lead the people into deeper understanding than he has himself. He is the proclaimer of God's Word, but he is first a hearer.

SPIRITUAL POWER

The preacher's hope of overcoming the barriers to his message lies in the ministry of the Holy Spirit to empower his preaching. Paul described his own preaching as going beyond the qualities of human rhetoric men might expect in a preacher (1 Cor 2). He said he did not come "with excellence of speech or of wisdom" (vs 1). In the first place the power of his preaching was not in an impressive *delivery*. The tradition of Greek and Roman oratory gave great weight

> *"The preacher, in all his weakness, boldly declares the Word of God in the power of the Spirit."*

to a dramatic presentation for effective public speech. Secondly, the power of his message was not based on intellectually stimulating *arguments*. Instead he simply declared and interpreted the story of Jesus and the cross (vs 2).

Paul's hope was that the response of the hearers would be faith (vs 5). But he did not want their faith to be a response to the wisdom of men. That faith must be in the power of God. Even though he preached "in weakness, in fear, and in much trembling," he expected his message to be accompanied by a "demonstration of the Spirit and of power" (vss 3, 4). Here is the divine-human mix again. The preacher, in all his weakness, boldly declares the Word of God in the power of the Spirit.

The wisdom of God is of a different sort than the wisdom of the world. The rulers of this age cannot fathom God's wisdom, centered as it is in the atoning death of Jesus on the cross. It is a mystery that has remained hidden to men from the beginning of history. God's wisdom is the *great alternative*, that vision of reality that the mind of man cannot grasp on its own. It is a worldview incompatible with the natural patterns of his thinking. It can only be revealed by the Spirit, for only the Spirit can search out the deep things of God (vs 10).

Man is handicapped by three problems in his natural thought processes, problems that keep him from grasping the truth of God (vs 9). First is the problem of *personal experience*: "eye has not seen." His understanding is limited by what he has himself experienced. If he has never "seen" it, he has trouble accepting it. Second, he is limited by the problem of *precedence*: "nor ear heard." If he has never heard of someone else experiencing this new wisdom, he cannot think it valid. Third, his grasp of the truth is limited by the problem of *perception*: "nor have entered into the heart of man." Due to his preoccupation with experience, he cannot even imagine the reality of God's wisdom. His mind cannot grasp it because it comes by faith in God. As a result, "the natural man does not receive the things of the Spirit of God, for they are foolishness to him" (vs 14).

God's wisdom can only be discerned spiritually. In the first place, only the spiritual man, born again to a new spiritual life, can understand the otherwise mysterious wisdom of God. Secondly, he can understand God's truth only as he is taught it by the Holy Spirit, who compares spiritual things with spiritual (vs 13). "No one knows the things of God except the Spirit of God" (vs 11). A third factor in the believer's discernment is the "mind of the Lord" (vs 16). The Christian cannot be taught by the Spirit if he is "carnal" (1 Cor 3.1). He must intentionally take on the attitude of Jesus (Phil 2.11), what Paul elsewhere called "walking in the Spirit" (Gal 5.16).

"Preaching is a ministry of the Spirit and the word through a yielded servant."

Preaching, then, is not a simple matter of declaring the ideas of the Christian faith. The preacher is not capable of understanding or communicating God's hidden wisdom without the Holy Spirit. It is only He who gives spiritual life, teaches spiritual wisdom, and creates a spiritual attitude in preacher and hearer alike. To say that preaching is a divine-human endeavor seems much too simple a formula. The preacher may think that divine-human means he can preach better with the help of God. More true to Scripture would be to say that preaching is a ministry of the Spirit and the word through a yielded servant.

A Great Cosmic War

Preaching in the purpose of God cannot be understood apart from the biblical view of an ongoing conflict between the forces of good and evil. Throughout the Scripture that cosmic war is woven into the fabric of biblical thinking as a backdrop for all that is said. The ministry of the Word of God involves engaging in that great conflict. It is a battle for truth against deceit, for the purposes of God against the wiles of the devil, for righteousness over sin.

The figure of light and darkness is often used in Scripture to picture the opposing forces at work in the world. In the creation account the earth is said to be "without form, and void; and darkness was on the face of the deep" (Gen. 1:2). The formless chaos, the emptiness, and the darkness are all the stuff with which the Creator works to bring order and fullness and light. "Then God said, 'Let there be light,' and there was light. Then God saw the light, that it was good; and God divided the light from the darkness" (Gen 1.3, 4).

John wrote that "God is light and in Him is no darkness at all" (1 John 1.5). Earth is a dark planet in rebellion against God, ruled by "the god of this age" (2 Cor 4.4) who sets himself against the "children of light" (Eph 5.8). Unbelievers are the captives of the ruler of darkness, whose minds he has blinded, "lest the light of the gospel of the glory of Christ, who is the image of God, should shine on them" (2 Cor 4.4). Believers are called "out of darkness into His marvelous light" (1 Pet 2.9). God "has delivered us from the power of darkness and conveyed us into the kingdom of the Son of His love" (Col 1.13).

Christ is the light that has come into the world, but "men loved darkness rather than light, because their deeds were evil" (John 3.19). Believers are commissioned to be a force for light in the dark world. Jesus told the disciples clearly, "You are the light of the world," like a city on a hill or a lamp on a lamp stand (Matt 5.14, 15). They are intentionally to scatter the darkness: "Let your light so shine before men, that they may see your good works and glorify your Father in heaven" (Matt 5.16).

> "Any time the Word of God is preached in the power of the Spirit, the enemy is engaged."

In this battle for truth and godliness, the Word of God is a powerful weapon. It is the "sword of the Spirit" (Eph 6.17), the one offensive weapon for engaging the "rulers of the darkness of this age, . . . spiritual hosts of wickedness in the heavenly places" (Eph 6.12). Paul's vision of this battle for the truth is clear: "For the weapons of our warfare are not carnal but mighty in God for pulling down strongholds, casting down arguments and every high thing that exalts itself against the knowledge of God, bringing every thought into captivity to the obedience of Christ" (2 Cor 10.4, 5).

Paul saw his own calling in terms of the war for light over darkness. He testified that Jesus sent him to the nations "to open their eyes, in order to turn them from darkness to light, and from the power of Satan to God, that they may receive forgiveness of sins and an inheritance among those who are sanctified by faith in Me" (Acts 26.18). Is not every preacher of the gospel called to a similar mission? Any time the Word of God is preached in the power of the Spirit, the enemy is engaged. The apostles knew this when they gave priority to "prayer and the ministry of the word" (Acts 6.4).

The Word of Faith

In the biblical view, the only appropriate response to the revelation of God is faith. This means that the aim of preaching it to make God known in order to call for a faith response in the hearer. Making God known and calling for trust in Him cannot be separated. That faith response will include acceptance of the truth of God and surrender to its requirements, confirmed by some clear action that makes the faith known to others.

"Without faith it is impossible to please Him," we read in Hebrews 11.6, "for he who comes to God must believe that He is, and that He is a rewarder of those who diligently seek Him." Any act of worship, obedience, or service must spring from faith in God or it is not acceptable to Him. Evoking a faith response is the basic purpose of God's revelation. He did not make Himself known to man to satisfy his curiosity. He revealed Himself so that man might trust Him.

It is this faith in God that puts man in a right relationship with Him. The righteousness of God, which is credited to man's account, comes only "through faith in Jesus Christ, to all and on all who believe" (Rom 3.22). The gospel of Christ is "the power of God to salvation to every one who believes" (Rom 1.16). The ongoing relationship with God through Christ is a matter of going "from faith to faith," for "the just shall live by faith" (Rom 1.17).

The method of communicating this saving revelation to man has been established by God Himself. The Bible is written to foster faith. John wrote specifically, "But these are written that you may believe that Jesus is the Christ, the Son of God, and that by believing you may have life in His name" (John 20.31). Paul poses God's communication problem in a series of questions in Romans 10.14–15.

- How shall they call on Him in whom they have not believed?
- How shall they believe in Him of whom they have not heard?
- How shall they hear without a preacher?
- How shall they preach unless they are sent?

This series of questions suggests the basics of God's plan for making Himself known to man and calling him to faith. A person will not call on God if he does not believe in Him. He cannot believe in Him if he has not heard of Him. He cannot hear of Him unless someone tells him of God. No one will tell him of God unless he is sent to do so. Paul's summary statement is clear, "So then faith comes by hearing, and hearing by the word of God" (Rom 10.17).

Preaching that is in harmony with God's communication plan will make its aim to call for a faith response in the hearer. The purpose of preaching cannot be to promote church causes. It cannot be to press for moral reform. It cannot be to push the preacher's agenda. Whatever the subject of the sermon, the underlying purpose must be to direct the hearer toward confidence in God. Without faith, no other response can be valid, for "whatever is not of faith is sin" (Rom 14.23).

> "Preaching that is in harmony with God's communication plan will make its aim to call for a faith response in the hearer."

Faith, as the New Testament presents it, is characterized in a number of ways that help further to clarify the preaching task. Biblical faith is *objective*, having its focus outside of man toward the credibility of the God who is beyond him. It is *cognitive*, based on the accuracy of one's knowledge and understanding of the nature and intentions of God. It is *supernatural*, as the truth is confirmed and faith is awakened by the Holy Spirit. It is *responsive*, calling for a specific and decisive response on the part of the believer to confirm his faith. It is *theocentric*, centered in the person and will of God, not in the experience of man. It is *effective*, bringing the grace of God to bear in the life of the believer. It is *relational*, essentially a personal confidence in the person of God.

Preaching that functions as an expression of the revelation of God will be designed in keeping with biblical faith. It will focus on the character and purpose of God, present clear theological truth, depend on the Holy Spirit, call for a faith response, point man away from himself to God, anticipate God's saving grace, and seek to relate the hearer personally to God.

PREACH THE WORD

Preaching is at the heart of the Christian ministry. Paul's charge to Timothy has been repeated for centuries as a challenge to the messenger of God. "Preach the word!" he wrote. "Be ready in season and out of season. Convince, rebuke, exhort, with all longsuffering and teaching" (2 Tim 4.2). The preacher is to declare God's Word when it seems timely, and when it does not. He is to give proof (*elegxon*), to reprimand (*epitimao*), and to encourage (*parakaleson*), and to do so as a patient teacher. The contemporary preacher hears the same charge echoing through the years past, "Preach the word!"

Preaching was central in the ministry of Jesus. He began his public ministry by preaching (Mark 1.14, 15). When He chose the apostles, He involved them in the preaching as well. "Then He appointed twelve," Mark reports, "that they might be with Him and that He might send them out to preach." Matthew wrote that He sent the twelve out with this charge, "As you go, preach, saying, 'The kingdom of heaven is at hand'" (Matt 10.7). Jesus later enlarged the corps of preachers to seventy and told them to proclaim the same message (Luke 10.9). Each of the four Gospels concludes with this commission to preach (Matt 28.18–20; Mark 16.15–18; Luke 24.46–48; John 20.21).

"Our sermons must be biblical, not only in content, but in other ways as well."

Six key New Testament words for preaching reflect the various shades of meaning that clarify the biblical concept. *Keryssein* (to proclaim) emphasizes not only the saving event of the cross but the saving impact of the proclamation of that gospel for the hearer. *Evangelizesthai* (synonymous with *keryssein*) points up the joyous nature of the message about Christ. *Marturein* (to witness) indicates that all true preaching must adhere to the apostolic witness. *Didaskein* (to teach) focuses on the theological meaning and practical implications of the message. The words *propheteuein* (to prophesy) and *parakalein* (to comfort or admonish) emphasize the need for applying the message to the particular situation of the hearers.[6]

The Bible is itself a proclamation of the word and deed of God in man's own experience. We come into very personal contact with the Word of God when we pick up a Bible and read it. The words of the Bible are the Word of God. The ideas in the New Testament gospels and epistles were first preached and then written. Authentic biblical preaching will find its model in the nature of the Bible. The biblical writers, as "preachers," show us that our sermons must be biblical, not only in content but in other ways as well.

The biblical writers tied their ideas closely to the Scripture they had. They focused on the character of God. They spoke to their own generation in their situation. They used vivid language and told dramatic stories. They wrote in faith, sincerely believing everything they said. Preaching that is biblical will follow the methods, attitudes, and faith of these biblical writers.

The Problem of Interpretation

A major challenge for the preacher is the interpretation of the text. Sermon preparation calls for interpretation to be intentional and scholarly. First the interpreter must carefully study the text for what it is. This is the question of *definition*, asking, "What is the nature of this text?" Second, he must discern out of the particulars of the text its timeless and universal meaning. This is the *meaning* question, "What does the text mean?" Third, he must consider the implications of the text's meaning for himself and his audience. This is the *significance* question, "What is the significance of this truth for me and my hearers?" While these questions fall naturally into this order, they are all relevant throughout the study of the text and preparation of the sermon.

17

The hermeneutical (interpretation) task is complicated by the differences between the contemporary world and the world of the biblical text—language, culture, worldview, religion, history, etc. Interpretation is largely a matter of bridging these distances with careful and diligent study.

An even more serious problem for the interpreter is his own subjectivity. The central issue in biblical interpretation is the *locus of meaning*, where the meaning is found in the interpretive process. Is the meaning in the text? Is it in the thinking of the original writer? Is it in the mind of the interpreter? Is it in the interaction of the interpreter with the text? Or should the preacher merely report the text and let the hearers find the meaning in their own response to it?

> *"A basic function of good hermeneutical principles is to help the interpreter overcome his own subjectivity."*

A basic function of good hermeneutical principles is to help the interpreter overcome his own subjectivity. Each of us has his mind already made up. We come to the task of interpreting Scripture with ideas about what it should mean, many of these ideas unstated and unexamined. These pre-understandings can so affect how an interpreter reads the text as to dictate its meaning. This is why one person sees one meaning and another something else. The *locus of meaning* in such a case is in the thinking of the interpreter rather than the words of the text.

The preacher's thinking is always a variable factor in the interpretive process. The constant factor is the text itself, in its words in their originally intended sense. These words do not change. That is the wonder of the biblical revelation. No matter by whom or when the text is approached the words are the same. It is the reader and interpreter that change. A faithful interpretation of the text requires principles and methods that allow the text to speak as intended and keep the subjectivity of the interpreter in check.

A thorough survey of hermeneutics is beyond the scope of this study. The faithful preacher will want to grow in this field of study throughout his life. Whatever his expertise in hermeneutics, he can begin with a sincere commitment to let the text speak and to interpret it as the original writer intended. Though this seems to be an elusive goal, there is no other place to start if we are to take the Bible seriously and let it speak as intended.

A Definition of Preaching

Now that we have considered some of the themes in a theology of preaching, what factors are necessary to a definition? Is there such a thing as authentic Christian preaching in comparison to which all other "preaching" is false to some degree? Though other factors might be added, a basic definition of *preaching* should include the following seven elements.

The first aspect of our understanding of preaching is *the revelation of God*. We have noted that preaching is God's idea, an ongoing expression of His revelation of Himself to man. Preaching springs first from the intention of God to make Himself known to man.

At the most practical level, preaching is *oral communication*. Various forms of media, simple and complex, can be used to communicate the truth of God. Though other forms of communication may carry the message, only as one declares God's revelation with the words of his mouth do we call it preaching. A sermon is a persuasive speech. It is much more than that, but it is at least that. Preaching is the most basic form of communication unique to man, spoken words for the hearing ear.

A third factor necessary to our definition of preaching is *the content*. There has been through the generations a great deal of variety in the content of preaching. In our own day it seems that preaching can contain whatever thoughts and words the preacher prefers. Authentic Christian preaching, however, should be based on the biblical text. It is only in the preaching of this authoritative word that the words of the preacher have authority beyond his own opinions. The content of preaching is essentially theological. It is about God, His nature, His purpose, His expectations, His intentions.

The identity of *the preacher* is another factor necessary to an understanding of Christian preaching. For one thing, no preacher is to declare the word of God on his own account. He must be called and commissioned to that assignment. Preaching the word of God is not like reading a radio commercial that has no connection to the life of the speaker. The nature of the Christian life is such that one may not

> ### Def·i·ni'tion:
> ### Christian Preaching
>
> Christian preaching is an expression of the revelation of God through oral communication, declared by a God-called messenger, by the enabling of the Holy Spirit, containing a theological message from the biblical text, addressed to a particular audience in their situation, with the aim of calling the hearers to faith in God.

rightly proclaim what he does not embrace by faith and live out in his own experience.

The dynamic that makes preaching effective is the ministry of *the Holy Spirit*. The Spirit is at work throughout the process of preparation and the delivery of a sermon, not only in the preacher but in the hearer as well. Though the word of God is inherently powerful, it is the Spirit who brings it to life in the preaching. The power of the word and the power of the Spirit are the same power.

The nature of *the audience* is so vital a factor that it must be included in our definition of preaching. In the absence of an audience there can be no preaching. It is for the hearer that God made Himself known. It is for the hearer that He calls out preachers. The attention of God's heart is to the one who needs to hear His word. The preacher will also give his heart's attention to that hearer. He will study and relate to his audience in the way most likely to evoke a positive reception for his message. He will address them as they are, in terms of their own particular frame of reference.

A final factor necessary to our definition of preaching is *the goal* of it. Why do we preach? What is our aim? What is it we hope will take place as a result of our preaching? We have said that preaching aims at a faith response. Since without faith it is impossible to please God (Heb 11.6), and faith comes through hearing the Word of God (Rom 10.17), it is vital that the preacher make his aim a faith response in the hearer. This will require an entirely different kind of preaching than many preachers are accustomed to doing.

What of the definition of preaching? Drawing upon the theological themes surveyed above, a definition might be written as follows: *Christian preaching is an expression of the revelation of God through oral communication, declared by a God-called messenger, by the enabling of the Holy Spirit, containing a theological message from the biblical text, addressed to a particular audience in their situation, with the aim of calling the hearers to faith in God.*

This brief discussion of the theological issues surrounding preaching does not by any means exhaust the subject. It does, however, give us a foundation for the practical treatment of sermon delivery that follows. Seeing the preaching ministry from the viewpoint of God's purpose helps keep the challenge of developing preaching skills in perspective. The ministry of preaching requires a lot of human effort, an openness to learn, a commitment to excellence, and a spirit of humility. It is appropriate, then, that we continue our study by examining the person of the preacher.

CHAPTER SUMMARY

The study of preaching can include homiletics, hermeneutics, speech communication, theology, and biblical literature. Preaching is best understood as a function of the revelation of God. Preaching exists because God has spoken and wants man to know what He has said. God's pattern for self-revelation shapes the nature and work of preaching.

Preaching communicates the living and powerful Word of God as we receive it in the Bible. But there are spiritual and cultural barriers which naturally hinder the communication process. It is only by the powerful enabling of the Holy Spirit that these barriers can be overcome.

Preaching is central to a primary strategy in the cosmic war of God against the forces of evil. The aim of preaching is to make God known and call the hearer to faith in God. Preaching is central to the biblical witness and the calling to ministry. Preaching the Word of God calls for careful interpretation of the biblical text as the primary source of revelational meaning.

REVIEW QUESTIONS

1. How is preaching related to the self-revelation of God?
2. How has God spoken to make Himself known to man?
3. How does the biblical concept of "word" differ from our own?

21

4. What are the barriers that keep one from hearing the Word of God?
5. What is the ministry of the Holy Spirit in preaching?
6. What does preaching have to do with confronting the forces of evil?
7. What are some of the shades of meaning indicated by New Testament words for preaching?
8. What is the central problem in biblical interpretation?
9. What is the author's definition of Christian preaching?

CHAPTER TWO

THE PERSON OF THE PREACHER

I n his classic and oft-quoted definition of *preaching*, Phillips Brooks wrote that preaching is "truth through personality." He explained his meaning:

> Truth through Personality is our description of real preaching. The truth must come really through the person, not merely over his lips, not merely into his understanding and out through his pen. It must come through his character, his affections, his whole intellectual and moral being. It must come genuinely through him. I think that, granting equal intelligence and study, here is the great difference which we feel between two preachers of the Word.[1]

As great a preacher as he was, Brooks's theology, his view of Scripture, his lifestyle, and his preaching would not be acceptable in an evangelical congregation today. His views were hardly acceptable to the Episcopal Church in his own day.[2] Nevertheless his Lectures on Preaching, presented in 1877 at Yale, ranks with the finest books on homiletics. His "truth through personality" definition has been quoted repeatedly in subsequent preaching books.

As much as I might prefer a definition that begins, "Preaching is a word from God," the "truth

"The preacher's personality has at least as much impact on the audience as the content of his message."

23

through personality" idea rings true. From the viewpoint of communication, it is obvious that the preacher himself has tremendous impact on whether the message is received. The power of oral communication (chapter 4) and the impact of nonverbal communication (chapter 6) will make that clear. Listen to churchgoers talk about preaching and you quickly realize that the preacher's personality has at least as much impact on the hearers as the content of his message.

Effective preaching as "truth through personality" calls for keeping the two factors in balance. Preaching that is out of balance toward the truth tends to minimize the personality of the preacher and is more academic and sterile, with little life impact on the audience. On the other hand, preaching that is too heavy on the personality side is probably weak in biblical authority and leaves the congregation more impressed with the preacher than the message. But when God's messenger and God's message are in harmony and the sermon is balanced with the divine word and the human voice, the preaching is powerful and effective.

In this chapter we will consider the significance for preaching of the person of the preacher. This not only requires looking into his spiritual life but examining other more mundane matters as well. I want to begin with the search for an adequate model for preachers. Then we will consider some factors of the preacher's background. Finally, the preacher's philosophy of ministry and attitudes will be explored.

A Model for Preaching

Like it or not, your own personality will so color your preaching as to be a determining factor in its effect with the audience. Who you are as a person is as important as what you preach. Christianity is such that the messenger cannot divorce himself from the message. Neither can he step aside and become invisible as he preaches the message. A salesman might sell Subarus while he drives a Buick, but the Christian preacher must allow the message to shape his life or he cannot preach. You cannot be one kind of person and another kind of preacher.

> "You cannot be one kind of person and another kind of preacher."

John Stott uses several biblical metaphors in his portrait of the preacher.[3] He describes the preacher as a steward, a herald, a witness, a father, and a servant. These are helpful models, as are shepherd, prophet, and priest. It takes several of these biblical snapshots, however, to complete the preacher's portrait. His task is larger than any one of them.

One model for preaching that brings a number of these metaphors together and centers in Christ is the incarnational theme. In the character of Jesus Christ as the child of a human mother as well as the divine Son of God, we see the two poles that create a continuing stress in preaching. On the one side is the "faith once delivered," the Word of God. On the other is the contemporary human situation, the particular context in which each sermon must be preached. Preaching, in this sense, is all human, and, at the same time, all divine.

Def·i·ni'tion:
The Incarnational Model

The person of Christ, as fully God and fully man, serves as a model for all ministry. In preaching this model portrays the two elements of truth and personality. The very Word of God is proclaimed by a very human agent. This is God's method of making Himself known.

John Stott entitled his preaching book *Between Two Worlds* to capture that tension between the world of the biblical revelation and the world of the contemporary audience. The preacher is caught between these two worlds. The Bible in his hand is the divine Word of God. But he is himself a part of this present age, a human messenger who clothes the word with his own personality in the sermon.

God has chosen to use such human agency, with all the risks and frailties that involves. In preaching, as incarnational, the word becomes flesh. Clyde Fant writes, "The incarnation, therefore, is the truest theological model for preaching because it was God's ultimate act of communication. Jesus, who was the Christ, most perfectly said God to us because the eternal Word took on human flesh in a contemporary situation. Preaching cannot do otherwise."[4]

Paul saw his ministry as incarnational, not only in the sense of God using him as His agent, but also in that Jesus was his model for every aspect of ministry. He wrote, "Imitate me, just as I also imitate Christ" (1 Cor 11.1). Though he struggled with his own humanity, he knew that the revelation of God would be communicated through such imperfect instruments as he was.

So it is the preacher himself at the center of the tension. He must balance truth and personality, the Word of God in Scripture and the reality of human agency in the present moment. He must be fully in touch with that word in its own historical context, understanding its message and trusting its authority. He must also be fully in touch with his own generation, understanding his audience in their need and himself in his own unique personhood.

LIVING WITH THE TENSION

This interpretation of preaching may seem to be at odds with the common desire of the evangelical preacher to "hide behind the cross." In his piety and his fear he longs to be somehow invisible so that nothing remains but the divine word. You have heard prayers such as, "Lord, let no one see this preacher today, but let everyone see Jesus." As I have complimented the sermons of young preachers, I have often been told, "It wasn't me; it was the Lord." My uneasiness with that view has occasionally had me say, "Well, it wasn't *that* good."

I realize that this "It wasn't me" statement is an attempt to give glory to God, but it is not really true to the reality of preaching. The tension we feel as preachers is between the divine word we handle and the very frail agents we know ourselves to be. But this tension cannot be resolved by removing either factor. If you give up on the divine and see preaching as a merely human activity, you have lost your message. If you give up on the human and try to hide your personality, you have lost the medium God has chosen to communicate to your generation.

The preacher is met with a dilemma. He wants his preaching to have the touch of God upon it. But he knows at the same time that he is a weak and damaged vessel. Paul understood this uneasiness with the worthiness of the preacher. "But we have this treasure in earthen vessels, that the excellence of the power may be of God and not of us" (2 Cor 4.7). His

> *"The tension we feel as preachers is between the divine word we handle and the very frail agents we know ourselves to be."*

desire is clear, that God be glorified and not man. So he saw the treasure of the Word of God as placed for safekeeping in mere household utensils. That is God's way, to use ordinary men in extraordinary ways in the proclamation of His word.

Whatever our sentiments about hiding our own frailty so that the perfect Word of God should come through, we are saddled with the reality of being earthen vessels in which God has placed His treasured word. This is God's plan. We must accept it. But not only must we accept it, we must come to terms with the prominent role of the preacher's personality in his preaching. Matthew Simpson wrote as a contemporary of Brooks, "The word of God is the constant quantity, the preacher the variable. If this be true, then that preaching is best which, on the one hand, is most full of the divine message, and which, on the other, has the greatest personality of the preacher."[5]

Who the preacher is comes through as a major element in the preaching mix. The preacher's identity colors all he says. It can give wings to the message and enhance it for the audience. It can also hinder the message and cause a reaction instead of receptivity. Who he seems to be as a person will impress the listeners as much as what he is saying.

Aristotle named three fundamental factors in persuasive public speech: *logos*, *ethos*, and *pathos*. These are the logical content of the speech, the character of the speaker, and the passion associated with the subject. Concerning ethos, he said, "Persuasion is achieved by the speaker's personal character when the speech is so spoken as to make us think him credible." He asserted that the speaker's character "may almost be called the most effective means of persuasion he possesses."[6]

More than the speakers Aristotle had in mind, the Christian preacher must not only declare but exemplify his message. There is a connection between his word and his walk that cannot be broken or all is lost. He is not an attorney arguing points of law. He is not a salesman pitching his merchandise. He is a messenger and a witness, whose persuasion is his own experience, whose appeal is his own commitment, whose teaching is his own practice.

THE PREACHER'S SPEECH PATTERNS

Very often we are able to identify a preacher's roots by the way he talks. Regional accents, vocabulary, and other signals tell on him. Warming himself at the fire of the enemy, Peter was accused of being associated with Jesus. "Surely you are one of them;" someone charged, "for you are a Galilean, and your speech shows it" (Mark 14.70).

Others come to quick conclusions about you from the way you talk. Those speech patterns have become so "normal" to you that you may have difficulty hearing how they sound to others. But just as you immediately assess another person by the way he or she talks, so others quickly and even unintentionally judge you by your speech. Your voice projects a mental image of who you are, regardless of how you look. Others will immediately discern whether you are from the local area, how much education you probably have, how you see yourself, and even whether they like you. For a preacher, this adds up to whether they are inclined to listen to you and take your message seriously.

> *"Like it or not, others come to quick conclusions about you from the way you talk."*

Three major factors are involved in a regional speech pattern. The most noticeable is what we usually call your *accent*, your particular way of pronouncing your words, along with the rhythm and the melody of your speech. By this accent you can often distinguish a person from the South, from New England, or from the Midwest. Sometimes you can tell whether a person is from one part or another of your own state.

A second factor in your speech will be your *articulation*. This has to do with how carefully you speak, how precisely you pronounce the consonants and vowels in your words. You may know what you intend to say, but what comes out may not be nearly as clear to those who hear you. After receiving my chicken order at a Kentucky Fried Chicken in North Carolina, the clerk asked, "YawgutchawCUUP?" I didn't understand what he was asking. After several repetitions of this same expression, he picked up the drink cups and handed them to me. What he meant to say didn't come out as intelligible to me.

The third factor others notice in your speech will be your *vocabulary*, the words you choose to express yourself. Do you say "y'all" or

28

"you guys" or "yous" for plural "you"? Do you go to the "coast" or to the "shore" (showuh) or to the "beach"? Do you "cut on the light" or "turn" it on or "switch" it on? Are you "about" to go to town or "fixin'" to go? These word choices all tell on you.

A regional accent can be a distraction to your preaching, or it can be a charming point of interest. Americans are usually fascinated by preachers from the British Isles because the accent adds interest and credibility to the sermon. A Southern accent can be welcomed in other parts of the United States because it is melodic and pleasant in tone. However, if the preacher slurs his sounds, mispronounces words, or uses odd vocabulary, his audience may think him ignorant, whatever his accent.

The first step in dealing with a regional speech pattern is learning to hear it in your own speech. Most of us really do not know how we sound to others. You may need help from someone who can point out how you are saying your words. A tape recorder will also be needed. After learning to hear how you sound to others, you can decide whether your speech patterns are a problem for your preaching. If so, you may want to learn what is called Standard American English, a general way of using American English without regional peculiarities. We will deal further with speech patterns in chapter 5.

Family and Church Background

Your family background is another major factor in shaping who you are as a preacher. You cannot be other than who you are, and your family experience is part of that identity. You are like your mother or your father. Sometimes it is a strange experience to stand a certain way or gesture with your hand and see your father in it. Somehow you know that is just the way he expressed himself. Your temperament

"A minister is expected to function in public with courtesy and grace."

has come from a long line of forebears. Your parents and grandparents set that pattern for you before you were born.

Your educational background also affects who you are as a preacher. In addition to your speech, your audience can tell by other means how well educated you are, by such indicators as your dress, manner, and social skills. Education is not determined by the number of years spent in school. Real education is a matter of knowledge, not only about the three *R's* but also of a wide range of subjects that are important to a modern minister. Education comes also from experience in various situations where you are exposed to ideas, customs, and manners beyond your own background.

A minister is expected to function in public with courtesy and grace. Preachers often come, however, from family backgrounds that are non-Christian or whose social and economic level gives little importance to such social skills. If a young minister's family background doesn't provide an education in the manner necessary for a Christian minister, he will have to learn it elsewhere. There is little appreciation or patience for a minister who is ill-mannered and crude because he knows no better.

Natural talents will also affect your preaching. Not all preachers are equal in the gifts appropriate for preaching. We all come with different voices, different tendencies as to movement, different sense of humor, different keenness of imagination. But each of us who is called to preach has talent sufficient for the assignment. We will not all be "stars" in the preaching galaxy, but we can all be faithful.

Spiritual gifts will affect your approach to preaching as well. If you have the gift of teaching, you may tend toward more research and deal more in concepts than in life application. If your gift is exhortation, you may want to lay out step-by-step instructions for the Christian life. If your gift is mercy, you may gravitate toward sermons that deal with the emotional ups and downs of life. If your gift is prophecy, you may have a strong motivation to preach the righteous judgment of God against sin.

Whatever your spiritual gifts and natural talents, you can guard against imbalance by a planned program of preaching from a variety of biblical texts. Expository preaching overcomes many of the weaknesses and biases of the preacher and offers the people a balanced diet of spiritual nourishment.

> *"We will not all be 'stars' in the preaching galaxy, but we can all be faithful."*

The church experience of the preacher also affects his view of preaching. Seminarians very often think of "church" in terms of their home church. If you grow up in a dynamic, growing church, you will likely have a more dynamic concept of worship and preaching. If your home church was characterized by a peculiar folk style or regional tradition, you will think of preaching in terms that fit that approach. Students from the mountains of North Carolina tell of the "hackers" from their region who preach in a unique style. Black students often come from churches where the preaching follows a traditional style that may not work well outside those circles.

Some students react against the preaching they heard in their youth. They may not know how they want to preach, but they know they do not want to preach the way it was done "back home." Their home church may have been spiritually lifeless and the preaching dull. They know there is a better approach but may not be sure how to accomplish it.

PHILOSOPHY OF MINISTRY

Every preacher has a philosophy of ministry, whether he realizes it or not. By *"philosophy"* I mean the general principles of a field of knowledge. By *ministry* I mean the vocational calling of the preacher and his function in it. So your philosophy of ministry is a set of general principles by which you function in your calling as a minister. Every preacher entering his ministry will have a philosophy of ministry. Even preachers with no experience or training will already have their own views at almost every point.

Areas of concern in a philosophy of ministry include your view of the church, the nature of the Christian life, the role of the pastor, the nature of preaching, the purpose of God in His call, how the church is to relate to the world, the moral life of the believer, and other such issues. In each of these areas you already have some opinions. In some you have strong convictions. In others you are open to discussion. Your views may be changing as you gain experience and knowledge. You may be able to give a strong theological basis for your views. Or you may realize you have just adopted the philosophy of others.

At whatever stage of development your philosophy of ministry is, and whatever its source, your preaching is dramatically affected by your views on these important matters. Your concept of what a sermon is and what it is supposed to accomplish will shape your preaching. Is the sermon a word from God? Does it require a basis in the biblical text? Is the preacher free to say whatever he wishes of his religious

31

views? Is the sermon to be taken as authoritative in the life of the church? Is it to convict, encourage, rebuke, counsel, warn, teach, frighten, build up, or tear down?

Def·i·ni'tion:
Philosophy of Ministry

Your philosophy of ministry is the basic assumptions you hold about your ministry and how you are to function in it. These foundational ideas can be unknowingly taken from conventional thought, or they can be carefully formulated on the basis of biblical truth and practical wisdom. The wise preacher will hold his beliefs about ministry tentatively, always ready to test each idea by the teachings of Scripture.

What of the relationship of the preacher to his audience? Is he in authority? If so, what is the nature of that authority? Is he best described as a prophet, a priest, a servant, a herald, or a pastor? Is he to remain somewhat aloof from the congregation, or is he to be one of them just like any other believer? Can he be open about his own struggles in the Christian life, or should he keep his weaknesses hidden lest his congregation lose respect for him?

One of the chief purposes of ministerial education is to help you formulate a sound, biblical philosophy of ministry. This requires a broad theological education including Bible, theology, history, and practical skills. It will call for critical thinking as you sort out various views. You will learn to reflect theologically on the practical challenges of ministry, applying biblical truths to life experience. You will formulate a picture of your role and calling that goes beyond the limited outlook of your background. But you will not forsake the convictions that brought you to Christ and caused you to surrender to His claim upon your life.

THE PREACHER'S EXAMPLE

I remember well as a high school and college student being called "preacher boy." I know the dear people in my home church and in the college church meant it as an expression of affection. I was even told by older preachers to "let the folks treat you like their children when you are young. They will like it. Do not try to appear more mature and experienced than you are." So I accepted the "preacher boy" label, but I didn't like it.

In my own mind I was much impressed with the fact that God Himself had called me to preach His word. I was called to preach just as surely as the prophets of the Old Testament and the apostles of the New. I was to be a man of God. This was a sacred calling and carried with it the promise of God that He would lead me and empower me for the work. What of it if I had no training or experience, didn't know how to prepare a sermon, and sounded like a teenager when I talked?

This calling to preach God's Word is such a personal matter. How can any of us be very objective about it? My calling and my sermons are so much an expression of my walk with God that I can become very sensitive about it. My own ego and my calling can be so intertwined that my pride is on the line in anything concerning the ministry. Instead of the ministry of Jesus Christ through me, it can easily become my ministry.

The attitude I take toward my own calling and how I am to fulfill it will have a dramatic effect on those to whom I preach. Deeper than attitude is the character God is building in me. If my own character is not based in biblical truth and I am immature in personal discipline, those who hear me preach will know it. There is no way to separate my own character and personality from my preaching. Who I am will have as much impact as what I say. The old saying is true of preaching: "Who you are speaks so loudly that I cannot hear what you say."

"There is no way to separate my own character and personality from my preaching."

Paul recognized this problem, especially on the part of the young preacher, when he wrote to Timothy. So he addressed the issue head-on. He charged his son in the ministry, "Let no one despise your youth, but be an example to the believers in word, in conduct, in love, in spirit, in faith, in purity" (1 Tim 4.12). The mention of such a thing as Timothy's youth in this way seems to suggest that he had a problem like any young preacher. Maybe they called him "preacher boy."

Whatever your age and experience as a preacher, the challenge in this verse is appropriate. These words are not just a string of virtues that sound good coming from an apostle. This charge to the preacher sets a direction for his own attitude and character development. But it is more than that. It is also precisely what is needed by the congregation if they are to have respect for the man and his message. Examine this verse more closely with me.

WORTHY OF RESPECT

First, Paul says, "Let no one despise your youth." This makes clear that Timothy was young, at least from Paul's viewpoint. It also suggests that some of the people may have thought Timothy too young for his assignment. The word, *"despise,"* which in our day can mean "hate," does not have that meaning here. Timothy may have hated at times being so young, but this word, *kataphroneo*, means "to disdain, to think little of, to hold in contempt."

Paul was addressing the real possibility that the people will not take a young preacher seriously. They might shrug him off and fail to listen to his preaching with the same respect they do an older man. People are naturally reluctant to show respect to the young who haven't proven themselves. On the other hand, they may respect their elders, those who are especially gifted or have accomplished much. That is the very problem. A young preacher has no gray hair and no accomplishments.

"At whatever stage of maturity you are at the moment, you can be a godly example."

So what is he to do? Is he to demand respect? Is he to claim special recognition by virtue of his calling? No. Paul was not telling Timothy to demand respect. He was telling him how to earn respect. The answer is simple: live what you preach. Beyond that, live it better than anyone else. If you are to have respect as a preacher, young or old, you must set the pace in the Christian life. You must be "an example to the believers." They will see your godly life and know you are worthy of a hearing.

An example, *tupos*, is a pattern to follow. Is it possible for a young preacher to be an example to older and more experienced believers? Yes, it is. This is one of the marvels of the Christian life. Whatever your stage of maturity at the moment, you can be a godly example. Even though you will continue to grow, you can earn respect and set a pattern for others to follow, even as a youth. In fact, you never outlive this need for exemplary living. Preaching the gospel calls for living the gospel. Let me say it again: you cannot be one kind of person and another kind of preacher.

Paul named six areas in which the preacher is to set the pace for others. The first is "in word." The preacher is to be exemplary in speech. Your hearers will not only note what you say in your sermons; they are also listening to what you say in everyday speech. They notice whether your speech follows Paul's admonition, "Let no corrupt word proceed out of your mouth, but what is good for necessary edification, that it may impart grace to the hearers" (Eph 4.29). Our speech must not be corrupt, rotten, and putrid like decaying fruit. Rather it is to be good, wholesome, and sound. It is to build up the hearers so that our very words minister the grace of God to them.

Second, the preacher is to be exemplary in "conduct," his behavior and manner of life. You can be sure that any believer calls for the spotlight on his life when he declares openly his commitment to Christ. This is especially true when one announces that God has called him to preach. The people expect the man of God to live a life above reproach in the sight of believer and nonbeliever alike (1 Tim 3.7). The congregation notices how the preacher treats his family, his courtesy to his wife, his handling of his children. They notice his manners, his lifestyle, his attitude.

The third area in which the preacher is to be exemplary is "in love." This love, *agape*, is the supreme mark of a Christian because it is the essence of God's own character. This is not an emotional response to others. It is rather a matter of intention and action. Christian love behaves with the interests of others in mind, to give them the good that God would want for them. The preacher will find those in any congregation who are hard to like, but he is under a mandate to love them. His credibility is on the line. How can he preach unless he lives out the love that "suffers long and is kind," that "does not envy, . . . does not parade itself, is not puffed up" and so on (1 Cor 13.4ff).

The preacher is also to be exemplary "in spirit." What does Paul mean here by "spirit"? In some texts this word in not included. It is, however, in keeping with the tone and purpose of the verse. A preacher should be an example in his zeal, the enlivening of his attitude and out-

35

look by the very Spirit of God. There should be a spirit in him of devotion and reverence, of respect and humility. If his soul is afire with a vision of God and His purpose, the congregation will hear his preaching with more attention and receptivity.

The fifth area in which the preacher is to be exemplary is "in faith." Thayer defines faith as the "conviction of the truth of anything," generally joined with the idea of "trust and holy fervor." Of all the qualities needed by preacher and hearers alike, faith is most vital to preaching. Faith is the overarching aim of every sermon. The one response intended for the preaching of the gospel is faith. Out of genuine faith comes obedience. If the preacher really believes God's Word and really trusts God to do everything He has promised, he is setting the right kind of example for the people, whatever his age and maturity.

The last quality Paul names in which the preacher is to set the example is "in purity." The word here is *hagneia*, meaning "purity, sinless-

---

The Preacher as Example

1 Timothy 4.12

Exemplary speech *(logos)* in and out of the pulpit.
Exemplary conduct *(anastrophe)* in every relationship of life.
Exemplary love *(agape)* as basic to Christian character.
Exemplary spirit *(pneuma)* in every attitude and expression.
Exemplary faith *(pistis)* for every challenge in ministry.
Exemplary purity *(hagneia)* without even the hint of sin.

---

ness of life." There is no place in the church for the stain of the world. The preacher is to avoid even the appearance of evil, that no circumstance in which he places himself cause doubt in this regard. An interview with the aging Billy Graham came to the area of scandal and moral purity. The interviewer pointed out that no hint of such had ever come up with Dr. Graham or any of his team. He responded that early on, as young men, he, Cliff Barrows, and George Beverly Shea had covenanted together about rules for conduct. A preacher can be respected only if he is pure.

There is much more to say about the preacher's character and attitudes. The truth is simple. Let me say it again: You cannot be one kind of person and another kind of preacher. At this point we must move on to an analysis of the audience the preacher will face. ꜰ

Chapter Summary

This chapter addresses the significance of the preacher himself for his preaching ministry. Preaching is "truth through personality." The incarnational model for preaching follows the character of Christ as the divine Word in human flesh. The preacher experiences the tension created by the dual nature of his calling, the divine word handled by a frail human agent.

The preacher's speech patterns affect his hearer's view of him as much as any other factor. His family and church background have shaped his personality and outlook. His philosophy of ministry is the set of principles that guide him in his ministry.

Whatever a preacher's age or experience, he is to be an example to the believers. He will earn the respect of his hearers by setting the pace in Christian speech, conduct, love, spirit, faith, and purity.

Review Questions

1. Explain Phillips Brooks's definition of *preaching*.
2. What model for preaching focuses on the experience of Jesus?
3. What tension does the preacher experience in his task?
4. What are Aristotle's three factors in persuasion?
5. How does a regional accent affect your preaching, and what can be done about it?
6. In what ways does the preacher's background affect his preaching?
7. What is a philosophy of ministry?
8. How can a young preacher gain the respect of his audience?
9. In what ways does Paul urge the young preacher to set the example?

CHAPTER THREE

KNOWING YOUR AUDIENCE

Think of the various factors in the preaching situation: the *preacher*, the *Bible*, the *sermon*, the *occasion*, and the *audience*. Which of these is the most important element? Would you say it's the *Bible*? After all, the Word of God is what we preach. Or is the most important factor the *sermon*? In most cases that's the reason for the meeting—to hear the sermon. How about the *preacher*? Without him there wouldn't be any sermon to hear. Or is it the *audience*? Without the audience, would any of the other factors be needed?

As you might already guess by the title of this chapter, I think the most important element in the preaching situation is the audience. Without the audience, there would be no need for the preacher and his sermon. Indeed, there would be no need for the Bible. Had there not been a world of people in need of a word from God, there would be no Bible. God's purpose for preaching is to speak to man. The audience is the key element in the preaching situation.

This chapter is about audience *analysis* and *adaptation,* the process of examining and using information about the hearers you expect to address. Your analysis will help you adapt your sermon so that your hearers are more likely to respond as you wish. Audience analysis is common in our everyday conversation. In the most informal chat

> *"Had there not been a world of people in need of a word from God, there would be no Bible."*

we try to "read" others and adjust to their interests and response. We analyze their attitudes, knowledge, biases, values, and other qualities so that we can adapt our messages to those with whom we are speaking. This is audience analysis and adaptation.

Most homiletics books concentrate on the philosophy of preaching and the subject and structure of the sermon, with little attention to the audience. In the study of speech communication, however, the audience is given a primary place in the public speech situation. As you will see in the course of this chapter, there is much to learn about audience analysis that will help your preaching.

Sometimes the preacher seems like a cook at a soup kitchen, dishing up bread and soup to a line of nameless, faceless vagrants who file by. The focus is on the food and whether there is enough for everybody. It is as though everything beyond the food containers and serving ladles is a blur. He knows there are people out there, but the cook's problem is not with the eating and the eater but only with the cooking and the food. A preacher who is so preoccupied with what he will say that he misses thinking about the needs and interests of his audience will probably not deal very well with either.

What Is an Audience?

What do we mean by the *audience*? For a pastor the audience may mean his congregation, or that particular segment of them before him on a given Sunday. For an itinerant preacher, the audience may change every week. Social psychologist Kimball Young has written that the main features of an audience are: (1) it has a specific purpose, (2) it meets at a predetermined time and place, and (3) it has a standard form of polarization and interaction.[1] Let's think about these qualities.

In a normal preaching situation the purpose is worship. Or is it? If a survey were taken and you could somehow read the real motivations of every person in the auditorium, what do you think would be the most common purpose for being there? Many might say, "To attend the service." But what does that mean? Are they there from habit? Are they there to socialize? Are they there out of a sense of religious obligation? According to Young, an authentic audience requires a specific purpose. If a worship service group has no common purpose, can it really be an audience?

The second element, time and place, are usually set for a worship service. Of course, you could preach on the street, with no advance planning and, thus, no real audience, unless you attract one. In a normal worship meeting, those present have all come to a specific place at a predetermined time. In that sense they would qualify as an audience.

"If a worship service group has no common purpose, can it really be an audience?"

Now consider the third quality of an authentic audience. What does "polarization and interaction" mean? *Polarization* means the process by which a collection of individuals in an auditorium becomes a group. They become an "audience" only when they consciously accept their role as listeners and the role of the speaker as speaker. Polarization means an otherwise unorganized group finds a common focus and purpose. Their common focus is the preacher and their common purpose is to hear his sermon. Even a church group accustomed to attending worship together is not an audience until they jointly accept this focus and purpose.

Young also asserts that a formal audience has a standard form of *interaction*. In a preaching situation, interaction will take place in two directions, between audience members and between audience and speaker. The interaction of audience members before the sermon can tell a preacher much about their relationships and attitudes toward one another, toward the church, and toward the meeting. The more compatible the audience members are with one another, the more predictable is their interaction and response. The more common ground they share, the more they will react in the same way to the speaker.

Making an Audience

Though these factors necessary to an audience may sound a bit too technical for practical use, let me describe how this works in a preaching situation.

A room full of people, even in church, is not necessarily an audience, not until they concentrate on the preacher and his message. You hope they will become an audience. You pray they will become an audience. But they may not actually become an audience until a few minutes into your sermon, if then. Your aim is to arrest their attention and keep their interest throughout your sermon. In reality you hope to make an audience of them, to keep them focused until the sermon is over.

Whether you are able to "make an audience" of your hearers is largely dependent on how well you know them. I don't mean you must personally be acquainted with each person present. I mean that you cannot speak effectively to people unless you have some understanding of them. Knowing your audience allows you to fit your message to their interests, your structure to their understanding, your supporting materials to their experience. Not only will you try to fit your sermon to your hearers as you prepare it, you will adjust what you are saying to their response as you preach.

> *"Even though they may be looking at the preacher, they only listen when the message touches their lives in some way."*

This kind of preaching might be called *audience-centered*. But that does not mean you aim only to entertain. Neither does that mean you are trying to please them in what you say. Audience-centered preaching does not compromise the truth of the message as you interpret it from the Bible. Your alertness to your audience rather affects *how* you prepare and deliver your message. To say your sermon is "audience-centered" means you are planning and delivering your sermon with the audience in mind.

No matter how important and urgent your message is, if the people seated before you do not listen, really listen, they will not be helped by it. People do not listen to ideas that have no interest for them. That interest has to do with the connection between the sermon and their own personal concerns. Even though they may be looking at the preacher, they only listen when the message touches their lives in some way.

TYPES OF AUDIENCES

H. L. Hollingsworth has formulated what has become the classic categorization of audiences.[2] He suggested five types of audiences: (1) pedestrian, (2) passive, (3) selected, (4) concerted, and (5) organized. As a corollary to these categories, Hollingsworth names five fundamental tasks of a persuader: *attention*, *interest*, *impression*, *conviction*, and *direction*. Each of the audience types calls for a different strategy and responsibility on the part of the speaker. The preacher does well to determine what kind of audience he faces and what that requires of him as speaker.

The *pedestrian* audience is the most casual and least connected with the speaker, like passersby on a street corner. The speaker's crucial task is to get attention so that they become an audience. Whether he communicates very much to them depends on his success in getting them to focus on himself and what he is saying. Anyone who has done street preaching knows the challenge of this kind of audience. Unfortunately, most street preachers I have heard make no effort to arrest attention, just ignoring the indifference of the people around them.

The *passive* audience is often a captive one, like those attending a college lecture or after-dinner speech. The speaker will usually have the initial attention of such a group, but his challenge is to awaken their interest in his subject. Some Sunday worship crowds are *passive* audiences, willing to try to listen just because they are in church but giving up on the sermon pretty quickly if their interest isn't engaged. The preacher may also face this kind of audience at a jail service or in the nursing home parlor.

The *selected* audience is an interested but not necessarily harmonious group of individuals who have gathered for some common and known purpose. This kind of audience is often found in a closed or semiclosed meeting like a political briefing for constituents of various points of view. The speaker before such an audience usually has their

Hollingsworth's Audience Categories

The *pedestrian* audience: the speaker's challenge is getting their attention.

The *passive* audience: the speaker's challenge is awakening their interest.

The *selected* audience: the speaker's challenge is to make an impression.

The *concerted* audience: the speaker's challenge is to arouse conviction.

The *organized* audience: the speaker's challenge is to give direction.

attention and interest but must make an impression on them if his speech is to be effective. The preacher will face this kind of audience in some worship meetings such as a midweek service or in a church business meeting.

The *concerted* audience assembles with a common, active purpose in mind, with sympathetic interest in a mutual enterprise. You will find such an audience in a preparation rally for a political campaign or an evangelistic outreach. The speaker's challenge for this type of audience is to arouse their convictions about the subject at hand. The preacher will encounter this kind of audience when addressing a highly motivated leadership group in the church. Some churches are of such spiritual vitality that the regular Sunday worship crowd is a *concerted* audience.

The *organized* audience is one in which the speaker has considerable control and authority and the group is fully focused on his directions. It is an *organized* audience when coaches address athletic teams or officers speak to military units. In such a group the lines of authority and division of labor are clearly established. The speaker's task is to give direction for the action to be taken. A preacher will face such an audience as he gives instructions for a neighborhood canvass or some other such group effort.

Understanding People

Knowing your audience must begin with a general knowledge of human nature. People are much the same the world over. Even with very different social customs, different languages, and different political systems, human beings still have the basic needs and desires of life in common. They want personal worth and recognition. They want to love and be loved. They want the freedom to control their own lives. They want a sense of purpose and meaning. They want security, a sense of moral integrity, and personal peace.

There is another side to human nature you must know if you are to preach effectively. Human beings have a basically self-centered slant on life. They are interested in themselves more than any other subject. Their dreams and desires are for self-fulfillment. They become angry when they do not get their way. They worry, they complain, they feel sorry for themselves, they are sometimes discontent and lonely. They have regrets, memories of words and deeds they wish had never occurred. They do not understand themselves because they often want to do better but seem helpless to accomplish it.

Understanding human nature has been the goal of serious scholars and researchers for generations. Anthropologists have studied the culture of great civilizations and obscure tribes to discover how they think and behave and perhaps to understand why. Missiologists have analyzed various cultural and religious groups to see how the gospel might be presented to each people group in the most effective way. Church Growth experts in the United States have spelled out in detail who goes to church and why and how to reach various groups of people with various methods and appeals.

> *"Knowing your audience must begin with a general knowledge of human nature."*

Generational studies have fascinated students of human nature in recent decades. Most preachers are familiar with the common terms— Boomers, Busters, Generation X. These designations refer to groups of people according to their ages. Since those in each group are about the same age, they have grown up under similar world conditions and, thus, have similar values and attitudes. Though descriptions differ from one analyst to another, the profile of the most common groups gives an interesting insight into the various audiences faced by the contemporary preacher.

Michael Sack writes that *Generation X*, born between 1970 and 1985, is the "feed me" generation who likes to retreat into small groups and needs unconditional acceptance and clear priorities. The *Busters*, born between 1960 and 1970, don't like guarantees, need relationships, peer philosophizing, and to become creatively involved in making a better world. A third group, the *Boomers*, are faddish and intellectually lazy. Born between 1945 and 1960, they are the "entertain me and earn me" generation, looking for spiritual direction, and needing self-definition and worth. Older adults, the *Seniors*, were born before 1945. They have skills and money and want to do something worthwhile. They have been called the "need me and show me" generation.[3]

Whatever the value of the various studies of human nature, the modern preacher will want to be an expert on the people who make up his audience. The role of the audience, with all their natural personal concerns, is not a passive one. They actively engage the preacher by responding to him and to his sermon, sometimes affecting his message from moment to moment by their often subtle feedback. Preaching is two-way communication. The wise preacher will be sure to know something about those on the other side of that dialogue.

Six Factors in Demographic Analysis

"The goal of audience analysis is to discover which facets of listeners' demographic and psychological characteristics are relevant to your speech purposes and ideas."[4] This analysis is done so that you can adapt your purposes and ideas to those factors. In this definition you can see two kinds of audience analysis traditionally used by speakers: *demographic analysis* and *psychological profiling*. We will consider several important areas of inquiry in each of these categories.

A pastor on a new church field may want to do a formal written audience analysis. In order to become acquainted as quickly as possible with his new congregation, he can assemble the needed information for a demographic analysis and psychological profile. Most preachers, however, will do a more informal mental audience analysis as they look over the gathering crowd prior to a service. In one sense every meeting of a church involves a unique audience, with a particular combination of people, a distinct time and situation, a different tone. Whether formal and written or informal and mental, audience analysis is as important as textual study.

> "Whether formal and written or informal and mental, audience analysis is as important as textual study."

Factor #1: Age. Various age groups have very different ways of looking at life, different interests, and different needs. Any preacher knows that an audience of teenagers, on the one hand, or senior adults, on the other, will call for different subjects and preaching styles. Knowing the age breakdown for the audience is helpful throughout the sermon preparation process and in the delivery as well.

Factor #2: Gender is another consideration, determining the ratio of males to females in your audience. Whereas men listen more rationally by thinking in terms of the goal at hand, women are more intuitive and more likely to think relationally.[5] The wise preacher will organize his thoughts to be heard by men and women alike. Alice Matthews pleads with preachers to remember the frame of reference of their female listeners as they plan their sermons. She suggests replacing some of those sports analogies with illustrations about sewing or music.[6]

Factor #3: Ethnicity. Different racial and ethnic groups bring very different life experiences to a preaching situation. They may also have very different expectations about preaching. Various groups follow different customs as to the part the audience plays in preaching. Some groups prefer a more formal speaking style, while others expect a constant interaction between preacher and congregation.

Factor #4: Religion. Though most preachers will speak to audiences of their own faith, it is well to know the general outlook of the congregation or group. Differences in theological outlook and religious customs, even within a denomination, can seriously affect how a preacher is heard. Regional differences also affect religious views and practices.

Factor #5: Education. Most larger congregations have a wide variety of educational levels among regular attenders. Smaller churches tend to have a more homogeneous membership. The preacher will want to adapt his sermon presentation to the needs of all educational levels. He can try not to speak below the interests of the well educated or over the heads of the less educated.

Factor #6: Socioeconomic status. Two factors are joined here, social status and economic status. In America these are usually inseparable. Even in a rather generic middle-class American audience, there can be subtle but significant differences in where everyone falls in the local culture. Jobs, neighborhoods where they live, and income levels all contribute to a group consciousness that will affect how an audience responds to your sermon and to you.

Three Factors in Psychological Profiling

An audience analysis will also take into account several psychological factors that characterize the audience, particularly their attitudes, beliefs, and values.

Factor #1: Attitude. What is the attitude of the audience toward the preacher and his sermon? Your hearer's attitudes carry an emotional baggage to your sermon. They already have their minds made up on any number of issues. As you get into your topic, you will find them to be negative, neutral, or positive toward what you are saying. Avoid being discouraged by the negatives, try to win over the neutrals, and do what you can to reinforce the positives.

Establishing credibility with your hearers is vital to effective preaching. The audience may be suspicious of the preacher because they do not know him or do not think he is qualified to speak. In that case it may be wise to spend a few minutes getting acquainted with informal comments that let the audience know who you are. The preacher may be a "stranger" if he is of a different race or culture, or even if he comes from a different part of the country. If the preacher is able to establish common ground with his listeners, they will relax and more readily accept him and his message.

The attitude of your audience is also reflected in their expectations. A sermon can instruct, inspire, or amuse. What does your audience expect of your sermon? In some situations there seems to be no tolerance for humor in preaching. But those groups are rare that do not enjoy a good laugh. Some churches want a "lesson" and take out pen and notepaper as soon as you begin. Some insist on the King James Bible, while others prefer a modern translation. Wherever you preach, it is best to ask about these preferences and adapt to your audience so that they will better receive you and your message.

> *"In one sense attitudes are the emotional baggage listeners bring to your sermon."*

Factor #2: Beliefs. A "belief" is an assertion of something as true or false in life, an idea about how things really are in the world. People come to their beliefs through firsthand experience, through what they have read or heard, by the word of authorities they accept, or even by blind faith. Since preaching presents a belief system based on Scripture, it will often challenge the ideas of your hearers.

At times your hearers may not realize their thinking is being challenged in a sermon. They may be willing to accept both your idea and theirs, even though the two are in conflict. At other times they may realize you have contradicted their beliefs and be stirred to think seriously about it. Some beliefs are *fixed*, reinforced over and over again in one's life and interaction with others. Others are *variable*, less well anchored because they have not been fully proved in experience.[7] Obviously fixed beliefs are more difficult for a preacher to change than variable beliefs.

Factor #3: Values. Values are habitual judgments by which we look at life and the world around us. Attitudes arise from one's values, and values often come from one's beliefs. Edward Steele and Charles Redding have identified seven core categories for American values.[8]

1. *Puritan and pioneer morality*: seeing the world in moral terms as good or bad, ethical or unethical.
2. *Value of the individual*: the primacy of individual welfare in government and interpersonal relationships.
3. *Achievement and success*: desirability of material wealth and success, with job and social achievement.
4. *Change and progress*: society is progressing and developing for the better; change is to be desired.
5. *Ethical equality*: spiritual equality of all in the eyes of God, and equal opportunity through education.
6. *Effort and optimism*: obsession with the importance of work; view that all obstacles can be overcome.
7. *Efficiency, practicality, and pragmatism*: higher regard for practical thinkers and doers.

You can see immediately from this list that most Americans hold to these values. Since preaching inherently appeals to biblical values as authoritative, the preacher will test all other value systems by the truth of biblical principles. If the preacher knows the core values of his audience, he can present the message of his text in such a way as to confront those values, while at the same time maintaining a positive relationship with his hearers.

The long-term aim of a biblical preaching program is to effect change in the congregation. That goal can be more specifically identified as change in *beliefs*, *attitudes*, and *values*. When these core assumptions move in the direction of biblical principles, hearers are experiencing what the Bible calls "the renewing of your mind" (Rom 12.2). This change in thinking then results in a change in behavior. As a preacher knows his people and adapts his preaching approach to them, he will find them much more receptive to such a change.

In the survey of audience analysis above, I have already pointed out several ways audience analysis leads naturally to audience adaptation. Chapter 9 of this book will deal in more detail with how to design sermons that connect with today's audiences. At this point I want to look at audience adaptation in terms of the interests and expectations of your hearers.

ADAPTING TO THE AUDIENCE

The speaker's aim for audience adaptation is to arrest their attention and keep their interest so that the message may be received. This is not always an easy task for the preacher. Spurgeon told his students: "To me it is an annoyance if even a blind man does not look at me in the face. If I see anybody turning round, whispering, nodding, or looking at his watch, I judge that I am not up to the mark, and must by some means win these minds."[9]

It is an exhilarating experience for the preacher when his audience is fully connected with him and his message. They look at him intently. They hang on his every word. They are one with him in the communication process, fully engaged, attentive, alert. He seems to be able to play them like a violin. As the common saying puts it, he has them in the palm of his hand.

But many preachers face an entirely different audience every Sunday. They are listless, bored, preoccupied with other matters, distracted. At first this inattention bothers a new preacher. After a while, however, he may come to accept it as normal. Preaching to a distracted and bored audience is like walking in a muddy bog. It takes all the energy you have, and you still seem to be getting nowhere. Many preachers just trudge along anyway, chalking up the boredom to spiritual deadness in the church.

"Preaching to a distracted and bored audience is like walking in a muddy bog."

The common assumption, however, is that the speaker, not the hearer, is responsible for maintaining attention and interest. However unfair that may be to the preacher, it is the way most of us would see it. Ask any church attender about his expectations.

Does he feel that it is his job to pay attention to the sermon, in spite of whether it is interesting? Or does he feel it is the preacher's job to present the message in an interesting way? You know the answer.

Remember that your commitment as a preacher is to be "all things to all men" as you adapt to your audience. You are willing to do whatever it takes to be a faithful messenger of the Word of God. If adjustments are necessary for more effective communication, the preacher will be the one to adjust.

THE HOPES OF THE HEARER

Every person comes to church with a lot on his mind. As we might expect, each one is fully preoccupied with his own personal concerns. Preaching is quite a challenge when you realize that each person in your audience lives in his own circle of personal interests. The problems of his week follow him to church. No matter how he might try to listen to your sermon, his mind is drawn back to his own personal concerns.

Spurgeon admonished his students to sympathize with their audience: "Recollect that to some of our people it is not so easy to be attentive; many of them are not so interested in the matter. . . . Many of them have through the week been borne down by the press of business cares. . . . Do you always find it easy to escape from anxieties? Are you able to forget the sick wife and the ailing children at home?"[10]

Although he is sympathetic with his hearers' apathy, the preacher still faces the challenge of breaking through it. His aim is to take his message past all the distractions to the heart of his audience. He hopes for a response, for drawing near to God, for trusting in His offer of grace. Week after week he must try to take his message around the barriers and clutter of life to the core of his hearers' mind and will. How is that to be done?

The following drawing shows the preacher attempting to get through to his hearer. The circle represents the life of the hearer, particularly his own personal concerns. Each of the spiral symbols represents one of his concerns: family, work, future, health, marriage, children, bills, recreation, and so on. These are the matters he has on his mind as he faces the preacher on Sunday.

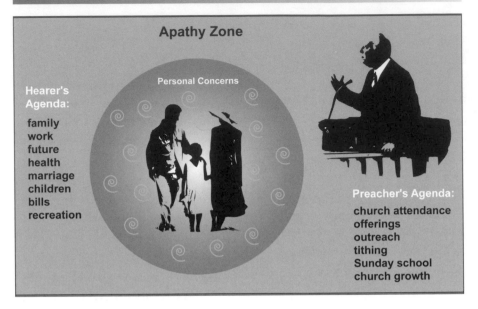

The preacher, on the other hand, has his own agenda. His role as pastor brings with it a set of responsibilities and concerns that shape that agenda. What is he thinking about? He is concerned with the success of the church. He is interested in tithing, attendance, outreach, moral integrity, faithfulness, Sunday school, the building fund, missions, and so on. No matter what text he chooses, his mind tends to gravitate back to these concerns as pastor. His agenda is to interest the people of the church in these matters so the church can prosper for the glory of God.

We can immediately see a conflict of interests. The man in the pew has a different set of concerns from the pastor. This puts the pastor and his preaching outside his circle of personal concerns, in the "apathy" zone. As he listens to the sermon he hears the "same old stuff," the same appeal for church faithfulness, witnessing, tithing, etc. It is easy to see why his mind wanders. He has enough to think about without taking on the preacher's concerns as well. Preachers have been talking about those things for generations, but his rebellious teenaged son is a problem for right now.

Is the person in the pew interested in that kind of sermon? Not much. He may occasionally hear a promising statement and sit up with anticipation. But in all likelihood he was mistaken. It was just an interesting story with the same old point. The trouble with sermons is that many of them don't have anything to do with anything. Most of the congregation is in need of a word from God for some personal concern, but the preacher is trying to get the believer to do something for the benefit of the church.

Spurgeon said, "In order to get attention, the first golden rule is, always say something worth hearing."[11] The question must then be asked whether the "something" of the sermon is worth hearing from the preacher's viewpoint or from the viewpoint of the hearer. It is obvious that the preacher might be intensely interested in church matters, but many of his listeners are too burdened with personal problems to pay much attention. Unless the subject of the sermon is of interest to the person in the pew, its value is questionable from a communication viewpoint.

This frustrates the pastor. He protests, "They *should* be interested in attendance and outreach and giving. They are Christians and this is their church. It is up to them to do the work of the church and keep its doors open." He may protest even more that they should be interested in the Second Coming of Christ, the meaning of the Tabernacle, and the heavenly visions of the apostle Paul. These are important themes. Christians should know this stuff.

"The people in the pews are indifferent about preaching when it does not connect with their lives."

On the other hand we might ask, "Does the Bible have anything to say about the personal concerns of the person in the pew?" Of course it does. The Bible speaks to man in every area of his personal life. There is good news of God's provision, His protection, His leadership, His presence. If the Bible speaks of these matters, why can't the preacher speak about them from the pulpit? Will that not arrest the attention and awaken the interest of his hearers?

When a believer is worrying about a lab report due next Tuesday, it is difficult for him to concentrate on subscribing the church budget. When a couple knows that they are drifting apart and that their marriage is threatened, they cannot generate much interest in the building program. Teenagers facing the constant pressure to forsake their convictions in an immoral world have a hard time getting into the plagues of the Apocalypse.

Please understand that I am not making light of any of these biblical themes or of the needs of the church in its institutional life. I am saying, however, that everything the Bible says must have a connection with human experience or it is apparently irrelevant to us. It is no wonder the people in the pews are indifferent about preaching when it does not connect with their lives.

An effort to understand your audience and connect with their interests must never compromise the biblical message. Audience analysis and adaptation is part of your communication strategy. But it must not be allowed to corrupt sound theology. Your audience needs to hear a word from God. Whether they really hear it may depend on how well you make the connection with their personal concerns.

Knowing your audience calls for both audience analysis and audience adaptation. In various other chapters we will touch on this subject again. Not only does the preacher adapt to his audience in his choice of a topic and how he develops it, but he also adapts to his hearers during the sermon. I will have more to say about this in our final chapter, "The Preaching Moment." Now, chapter 4 will explore the challenge of oral communication.

Chapter Summary

The audience is the most important of the elements involved in the preaching situation. Audience *analysis* and *adaptation* is the process of examining and utilizing information about the hearers you expect to address. An audience is marked by purpose, time, and place for meeting, and certain relationships with the speaker and one another. The preacher aims to "make an audience" of the assembled crowd. Different kinds of audiences call for different tasks on the part of the preacher.

Audience analysis generally deals with the *psychological* and the *demographic*. Demographic analysis considers age, gender, ethnic and racial background, religion, education, socioeconomic status, and other such factors. Psychological analysis examines attitudes, beliefs, and values.

The preacher will adapt to his hearers by understanding their experience. They will be interested in a sermon only if it touches their lives at some significant point. The preacher might have an institutional agenda, but he is wise to adapt to the needs of his audience.

REVIEW QUESTIONS

1. Why is the audience the most important factor in the preaching situation?
2. What is meant by "audience analysis"?
3. How does Kimball Young define an audience, and what does he mean by *polarization* and *interaction*?
4. What does it take for an auditorium full of people to become an audience?
5. What are the five types of audiences identified by Hollingsworth?
6. What can a preacher know in advance about any audience?
7. What are two basic kinds of audience analysis?
8. Identify three methods for gathering information about your audience.
9. What demographic factors might be considered for analyzing your audience?
10. What can the preacher do to improve the attitude of the audience toward himself?
11. How do your audience members acquire their beliefs?

CHAPTER FOUR

THE CHALLENGE OF ORAL COMMUNICATION

H uman communication is a complex and mysterious phenome-
non. The effort to communicate is so much a part of our everyday living that we do not think much about how it is possible
and what is actually happening. In the information age, however, the concern of man with how to communicate has become a constant priority.
Today, instant communication takes place on a worldwide basis. Through
telephone, radio and television, satellites, and computers, the extent and
speed of communication has expanded beyond imagination.

Def·i·ni'tion:
Communication

The word *communicate* comes from the Latin word *communi-
care*, which means "to impart or share," and that from the word
communis, meaning "common." The root idea of communication
suggests that it is a process by which we impart ideas one to
another. The aim of communication is the holding of ideas in common, understanding them with the same meaning.

Though oral communication is only one division of a vast field of
communication studies, it is the foundational area. The gift of speech
distinguishes man from all other animals in God's creation. Man communicates through speech as his primary link with his fellowman. It is
the *oral/aural* medium. *Oral* means "by mouth" or "spoken" and,

when linked with *communication,* refers to human speech. *Aural* has to do with the ear and hearing. So *oral/aural* means a spoken message for the hearing ear. I will often use the term "speech communication" as synonymous with "oral communication." I like James Henning's definition of oral communication. He writes, "Oral communication is the integrated use of words, voice, and action by the speaker for the purpose of accurate and skillful communication of his ideas and feelings to a listener."[1]

For the pastor, oral communication is his most important function. Not only does his weekly preaching ministry require much of his time and attention, he is communicating in every other pastoral responsibility as well. In administration, in counseling, in personal evangelism, in prayer, in relationships with his people, in his leadership—oral communication is the business of the minister.

In this chapter we will consider the challenge of oral communication. After a look at some false assumptions about speech communication, we will examine the various elements that make up the communication process. Then we will note how the communication process seems to break the bounds of our efforts to describe it. Finally, we will look at the various levels at which oral communication takes place.

Mistaken Assumptions

Human speech is as common as anything about us. It seems that everyone can talk, however limited or elaborate his manner of expressing himself orally. The pervasiveness of oral communication makes us all think we know a good bit about it. We have been talking since we were babies. It is as normal as breathing. We rarely have to think about it. We just open our mouths, and the words come naturally. We hear speech all day, if not in conversation with others, in the background as others talk at the office, over radio and television, at school, everywhere.

"The pervasiveness of oral communication makes us all think we know a good bit about it."

Speech communication is a field of study to which teachers, researchers, and scientists have devoted their lives. The new ground in this study is still being explored. There is yet a lot of disagreement as to how we should understand and explain various aspects of human communication. Think with me about some of the common assumptions about speech, particularly preaching. Though they sound reasonable, they are faulty in important ways.

Misconception #1: Since anyone can talk, there is little need for training in speech communication. Though most of us would be reluctant to admit it, we assume this is largely true. I often speak with incoming seminary students who have been preaching already, some for years. I usually ask what training they have had in speech communication, particularly in preaching. Very often they have none. One student even told me he did not want to take preaching because he was already a very good preacher and did not want to risk being corrupted by the course.

A university speech teacher told me that her basic course, though required in the curriculum for most degrees, was thought by many of the students to be a waste of time. What can there possibly be to learn about how to talk? Speech training is lumped in the same category with the arts—with music, dance, sculpture, and drama. Only a small group of specialists ever need to study these subjects. As we will see, however, there is more to learn about oral communication than most of us can grasp.

Misconception #2: Speech communication is simple: someone talks and someone hears what he says. Simple communication transactions like this take place dozens of times every day for most of us. We hardly think about what is happening. A closer look at the communication process, however, will show us how complex and mysterious this simple transaction is. We catch a glimpse of the mystery of human speech when it doesn't work as intended. "I didn't say that!" "Yes, you did. I distinctly remember your telling me this." "I think I should know what I said or didn't say." And so on such conflicts can go.

Misconception #3: Words say what they say, and we all know what they mean. Words do have meaning. We give them the meaning we intend them to carry in normal conversation. But that meaning can vary from one person to another. Besides that, the attitude of the speaker and his relationship with the hearer can give the words a twist that changes the meaning. The oral communication process is much more than words, as we will see in chapter 6 when we examine the many channels of nonverbal communication.

Misconception #4: Any reasonably intelligent person can express what he means to say. This assumption seems true enough until you think about how important the listening side is to speech communication. You know the experience. You are trying to explain your thinking on a certain subject or tell a story of some experience. Then you get the uneasy and irritating feeling that the person you are talking to isn't listening. This is especially discouraging in preaching. But most preachers can look at faces in their audience and know they are "tuned out."

> *"Some preachers think that God will make them skilled communicators just by virtue of their calling."*

Misconception #5: A preacher usually is born with the "gift of gab" and does not have to study how to speak well. Many believers think that preaching is a calling that makes the preacher immune to the normal fear and stumbling connected with making a speech. On the other hand, they know very well that some preachers do not have the skill to communicate effectively. Worst of all, some preachers think that God will make them skilled communicators just by virtue of their calling. The gifts and talents for ministry are always a partnership. God gives them, and the minister must develop and exercise them. Preaching is a divine/human endeavor that requires the preacher to develop his skills in every way he can while depending on God to make his preaching more than mere human speech.

Misconception #6: Preaching is a simple matter of declaring the message and trusting the Holy Spirit to put it across. The role of the Holy Spirit in preaching is vital. Without the work of the Spirit, there can be no authentic preaching. As we have already seen, however, God has decided to communicate with mankind through human agency. He calls out messengers and trusts them with His word to this needy world. The work of the Holy Spirit does not mean that the preacher should not try to develop skills for effective speech and learn how to persuade his audience every way he can.

Misconception #7: The preacher should just be himself and let the audience adjust to his way of talking. Most preachers take this viewpoint even without planning to do so. They are usually so wrapped up in their sermons that they do not think much about the audience. Being yourself in your preaching is very important for effective communication. A genuine and sincere manner of speech gives the hearer more confidence in the preacher. But another principle calls for the preacher to adjust to his audience in order to get the message across to them. Remember, we are committed to being "all things to all men."

These misconceptions about preaching can be overcome as we better understand the biblical view of our calling and the complex nature of oral communication. As servants of God, we want to serve Him on His terms, not ours. We want to take advantage of everything we can learn about effective speech. Our calling requires our best. Now let's consider the complex process of speech communication.

The Communication Process

The communication process has long been portrayed with "models" designed to picture how the various elements work.[2] The most basic model will include at least four elements: the *sender*, the *receiver*, the *message*, and the *channel*. In the simplest way of describing oral communication we can say that one person (the *sender*) puts his idea (the *message*) into words (the *channel*) for another (the *receiver*) to understand.

This is a "cybernetic" model that grew out of modern telecommunications technology. The way communication media function provided a way to talk about human communication. This cybernetic model has become so widely used now that communication is generally understood in these terms.[3]

The *sender* is the speaker whose person, behavior and words communicate meaning to those around him. As we have already discussed, the person of the preacher is a vital factor in God's plan for preaching. Not only is the delivery skill of the preacher important, his physical appearance, his character, his personality, his attitude—everything about him is involved in his preaching. Preaching is not only something he does; it is something he is. Message and messenger cannot be easily separated.

The *receiver* is the one or many who perceive the signals of the speaker's communication and discern meaning from them. Our study of the audience revealed what a complex challenge they present to the preacher. The hearer of a sermon is obviously not a passive receptacle into which a message can be tossed whole. He is a complicated individual who hears every word in terms of his own perspective on life.

The *message* is the meaning communicated by the various signals sent and received. The message is identified here as *meaning* rather than *information*. It is important to see the message in these terms. People are not computers who dispassionately transfer data. They are subjective thinkers who can only communicate in terms of their own experience. The ideal for speech communication is to have the message in the speaker's thoughts be duplicated in the mind of the hearer. Even when the best possible conditions prevail, however, communication is probably only about 80 percent effective.[4] The preacher can only hope that the essential elements of his message are communicated accurately most of the time.

> *"The preacher is using many more channels than he even realizes and sending messages whether he intends to or not."*

The *channels* are the means by which the signals are sent and received. At the most basic level, these channels are sight, hearing, touch, and smell. These are the senses by which we perceive signals from others. At another level we can think of channels as the kind of signals we send and receive. For oral communication we may discuss the channels as words, gestures, facial expressions, bodily movement, and other factors about the speaker. The preacher is using many more

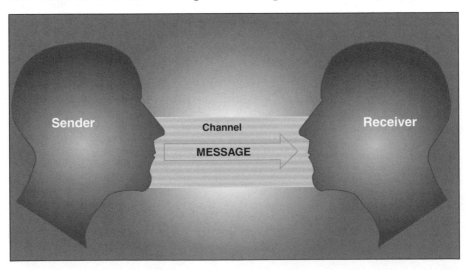

channels than he even realizes and sending messages whether he intends to or not.

We can begin our look at the communication process, then, with these four basic elements: a *sender*, a *receiver*, a *message*, and a *channel*.

A closer look at human communication, however, reveals that other elements are involved. In the first place, we know that both the sender and the receiver must relate meaning to the signals. This is called *encoding* and *decoding*. In one sense all communication is in code. The words and actions of the speaker are only understandable to someone who knows the code—the culture and language of the speaker. This coding is obvious when Americans have unknowingly used hand signals like the "thumbs-up" or "A-okay" signs in other countries where these are considered vulgar insults.

All language is code. But it is not usually intended to be a cryptic (hidden) code. It is intended to allow those of a common culture to communicate effectively with one another. Even within a culture, however, a person can easily misread the intention of the speaker from certain words or gestures he uses. The speaker must choose his signals carefully in terms of the common use familiar to the audience.

The sender, or speaker, translates his thoughts into words or actions (*encodes* them) and sends them as signals to the receiver. In other words he assigns meaning to these signals. The receiver then must also translate, or discern meaning in those signals (thus *decoding*) as he receives them. The aim is to have the same meaning understood by both. If the speaker and the hearer associate the same thought with the words and actions, the message has been sent and received.

> "In one sense all communication is in code."

Another element, *feedback*, should also be added to our model. It is obvious that communication is never limited to one direction. All parties both send and receive. In a conversation you take turns talking and listening. If one person so dominates the conversation that the other can say nothing, the silent party will communicate without words, in body language. He may also communicate by walking away. Even in a public speech situation such as preaching, the audience is continually sending feedback to the speaker, verbally and nonverbally.

Feedback allows the speaker to adapt to his audience during the speech itself. He is constantly monitoring their verbal and nonverbal signals for indications of interest, confusion, support, enthusiasm, apathy, and other responses to his message. This feedback completes the communication loop. The message goes out to the hearer, and the acknowledgment comes back to the speaker that the message has been received.

Negative factors in the communication process are called *noise*. Just as actual noise can be a hindrance to good oral communication by distracting the hearer, there is *noise* other than sound. *Noise*, in communication theory, is any distraction that interferes with the communication process. *Noise* can be sounds, sights, or unusual behavior, anything that hinders the reception of the message. Noise can be external to the hearer, in the circumstances or the speaker's manner. It can also be internal, in the hearer's own attitudes and thoughts.

A continuous challenge for any preacher is to identify and remove distractions in your own manner. Your language, your gestures, your use of notes, your tone of voice, your platform movement, your clothing, your accent—all of these and many other factors can be a source of *noise* to your audience, distracting them from your message. If you are committed to your calling, you will be willing to do whatever it takes to see that there are no distractions in your presentation of the biblical message. We will look more closely at some of these distractions later in this study.

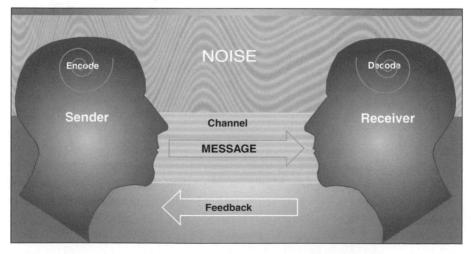

The elements in the communication process are now these: *sender, receiver, channel, message, encoding, decoding, feedback,* and *noise.* These new elements can be added to our diagram as follows:

Let's add to this model two other elements in the communication process. The first is the *field of experience* of those involved in the sending and receiving of messages. Every aspect of our communication is affected by our past experiences, our feelings, our attitudes, our knowledge, etc. All of this is our field of experience. If you have common ground with your hearer, there is a much better opportunity for "connecting" with him. If your fields of experience have no common ground, communication is all but impossible.

It is vital as a preacher that you understand yourself. Your own *field of experience* will shape your preaching more than your realize. In slang this is what is meant by "where you're coming from." In your preaching you will be yourself, and God intended that. But you will want to be your best self, the person and the preacher God is making of you. An objective understanding of all you bring to the preaching ministry from your past will make it possible to see yourself from beyond your own biases and allow God to shape your ministry and your preaching as He will.

It is also very important that a preacher understand the *field of experience* of his audience. As we have already considered in our discussion of audience analysis, you can minister the Word of God to an audience much more effectively if you know them. Just as you can move physically to another place in the room to get another perspective on the picture you have just hung, so can you mentally move to the position of your hearers and see things from their viewpoint. Your knowledge of yourself and of them will allow you to understand the common ground that can open the way for good communication. You will present to them the truths of Scripture set in the framework of their own lives.

An American pastor was preaching through an interpreter in Romania. He used in his sermon an extended illustration about playing golf. The local translator knew that there were no golf courses in Romania at that time and that the audience had little or no idea what the preacher meant. After attempting to fill in this gap of knowledge himself for a while, the interpreter finally stopped the preacher and explained that the audience didn't understand him. He had failed to take their field of experience into account in planning his sermon.

Another important factor for communication is *context*, the situation or environment in which the communication occurs. This can include the physical setting, the attitudes and expectations of participants, the time available, the mix of participants, the emotional climate, and other circumstantial factors that are a part of the communication situation. For a preacher the *context* is a vital element. He hopes the circumstances surrounding his sermon will enhance the reception of the message and not hinder it.

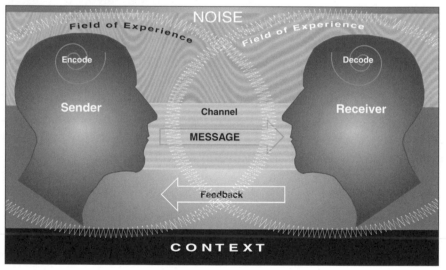

Now look closely at our diagram again, this time with two more factors added—*field of experience* and *context*.

The nature of the *context* will be a major factor in determining the best approach for any sermon. A more formal worship service may call for a certain kind of sermon preached in a certain way. So it is with a youth rally, or a jail service, or a open-air meeting in a foreign country. All the factors in the *context* will never be known to the preacher. They are too many, too subtle, and too complex. Not only are you facing the challenge of the physical context, you must also consider the emotional, historical, cultural, and philosophical contexts. You will want to analyze the situation as best you can for what you can discern about it. As we have said, the preacher does not compromise the message, but he is always ready to adapt it.

BEYOND THE SIMPLE MODELS

As the diagrams make clear, communication is a complex process. It is even more complex than this model suggests. Here we have only seen one side of the communication story. We have seen the speaker sending a message and the hearer acknowledging its reception with feedback. This model pictures communication as something like a game of pitch and catch. One person pitches the ball and another catches it. At any given moment it is a one-way process. But is normal communication really like this?

The straight arrow on our diagram shows the message being sent. In normal conversation the process is nothing like a straight line. Even adding the feedback line does not adequately picture the process. In reality signals are flying back and forth all at once. Not only the verbal, but also the many channels of nonverbal communication are in the mix. Rather than a simple game of pitch and catch, normal human communication is more like having a number of balls in the air at any moment, going in both directions. Messages are being sent and received with the speed of light.

This process becomes all the more complex when more people are involved. The preacher stands before an audience of dozens or hundreds, even thousands. Imagine how it would look if every message, verbal and nonverbal, were suddenly visible as a beam of light traveling between persons. See the beams as colorcoded to indicate the attitude of the sender. Red might be enthusiasm, blue indifference, yellow hostility, and green agreement. What a light show a normal sermon would produce!

"Speaking and listening are not separate activities taken in turn, but going on continuously."

We may think of communication as *action* in which one person sends a message and another person receives it. Our first diagram pictures this simple understanding. Communication can also be seen as *interaction*. One person sends a message and another receives it, who responds with another message. This is more like the game of pitch and catch. It is more realistic, however, to see the communication process as *transaction*, in which the communicators simultaneously send and receive messages. In this view, speaking and listening are not separate activities taken in turn, but going on continuously.[5]

For preaching, however, even the transactional model does not adequately cover the communication process. The elements we have named thus far are important but do not complete the picture: *sender, receiver, message, channels, encoding, decoding, feedback, noise, context,* and *field of experience.* All of these elements address speech communication on a human level. They do not take into account the vital factor of divine involvement.

Preaching, however, is a divine-human endeavor. Authentic preaching is the proclamation of the Word of God by the power of the Spirit of God. This power is not just zeal on the part of the speaker or inspiration and motivation in the interaction between speaker and audience. The activity of God in the communication process is not an emotional element, though it may be manifested by emotion. The Spirit of God is involved throughout the process to make an authentic sermon more than a speech, to make it an encounter with God.

Inexperienced preachers often feel vulnerable and ill equipped as they stand before the searching eyes of an audience. Preaching is one of the most important tasks any person can attempt. Eternity hangs in the balance for the hearer of God's Word. No wonder the preacher cries out to God with Paul, "Who is sufficient for these things?" (2 Cor. 2.16). But we are not in this alone. The promise of God's involvement in the proclamation of His word is a great source of encouragement to the preacher.

The Spirit of God is at work in the life and thinking of the preacher—to direct his thoughts, to inspire his interpretation of Scripture, to give him creative ideas for presenting the biblical message to his audience. The Spirit is also at work in the hearer—to testify to the truth of the biblical message, to illumine his thinking for understanding the message, to awaken his conscience to the conviction of sin and need, to give the gift of faith. The encoding and decoding are done with the touch of divine inspiration. The Spirit even works to close out distractions when the Word of God is preached. The Holy Spirit is the key element in the communication known as preaching.

> *"The Holy Spirit is the key element in the communication known as preaching."*

The complexity and wonder of the oral communication process makes it obvious that it is God who has given the gift of speech. The preacher who would be heard will want to understand that process as clearly as possible. Now let's consider how communication can take place at various levels.

LEVELS OF COMMUNICATION

Levels of communication can be understood in terms of the audience, its size and makeup. At the most basic level is *intrapersonal* communication, the inner conversation one has with oneself. In one sense this is the most important communicating you will do. In your ongoing conversation with yourself, you interpret what is taking place around you, think through how you will respond to it, and try out various approaches mentally before you speak or act.

The next level of communication is *interpersonal*. Whereas *intrapersonal* means within the person, *interpersonal* means between persons. At the most basic level, interpersonal communication is one-on-one. It involves two persons listening and speaking, alternating in these roles. It can range from the intimate and informal conversation of lovers to the formal and structured patterns of an interview. Effectiveness at other levels of communication will largely depend on learning the skills of interpersonal communication.

Communication in *small groups* is another level. This is a type of interpersonal communication. Though not exactly *dyadic* (two people one-on-one), small-group communication still carries the give-and-take of a conversation. Think of small-group communication as ranging from three to ten or twelve persons. It can be informal, like a family gathering around the table, or formal, like a board meeting. The minister's job calls for a variety of occasions when communication is at the small-group level. It is vital to know the dynamics and principles of effective small-group communication.

For the preacher, *mass* communication is important because at this level he reaches most of his flock through his preaching and teaching ministry. Mass communication usually means a dozen or more in the audience, with a more formal arrangement in which the speaker does the talking and the audience does the listening. It loses some of the conversational qualities of interpersonal and small-group communication. I have intentionally converted a meeting from mass to small-group when the audience was small enough. This simply required

Levels of Communication

Intrapersonal communication—your inner conversation with your-self.

Interpersonal communication—one-on-one between two persons.

Small-group communication—from three to ten persons interacting.

Mass communication—speaker/audience situation of twelve or more.

Intercultural communication—across language and cultural barriers.

Organizational communication—between persons in organizations.

having them sit in a circle instead of in rows facing the speaker and making it a discussion rather than a speech.

Mass communication can be either *public* communication, in which a person designated as the speaker addresses a group generally designated as listeners, or *broadcast* communication, in which the speaker addresses his audience over the medium of radio or television. This study will deal primarily with what has traditionally been called public speech. This is the level of communication at which preaching falls. Effective public speech draws heavily on the principles for good communication at the interpersonal level.

Two other levels of speech communication do not relate to the size of the audience so much as to the nature of the relationship between speaker and audience. In *intercultural* communication the speaker is addressing another or others across cultural and/or language barriers. Preachers can experience the need for intercultural (or cross-cultural) communication in a number of ways. Missionaries must deal with cultural differences that create barriers to effective communication. A preacher can also find it necessary to cross cultural barriers when facing an audience unlike the people of his home region. Most modern nations are made up of many subcultures with very different accents, vocabulary, and customs.

"There are many reasons we would rather talk than listen, most of them not good ones."

Organizational communication is another type of communication based on the speaker's relationship with his audience. Special attention has been given in recent decades to the way we communicate within structured organizations. A pastor will want to learn how to communicate well in the church, through all the channels available. One of the common complaints of church members is that communication is weak in the church, with some needed information not getting to all those who should know.

Though each of these levels of communication is described in terms of the speaker, nothing is more important than listening. In fact, listening must come before speaking. As we have heard repeatedly, "God gave you one mouth and two ears. Does that tell you anything about how much talking you should do and how much listening?" There are many reasons we would rather talk than listen, most of them not good ones. The preacher of God's Word who will be effective with any kind of audience will learn first to be a listener and then adapt the message to what the audience is saying.

Preaching may be much more than mere oral communication, but it is not less. The preacher will function in terms of the elements of oral communication consciously or unconsciously. Being serious about developing preaching skills means trying to understand the dynamics of the communication process. Preaching is first a science and afterward an art. The complexity and mystery of preaching call for a lifelong commitment to growth and discovery. Understanding the process of oral communication is a basic part of that commitment.

Basic also to your understanding of oral communication is the amazing process of vocal production which we will consider now in chapter 5.

Chapter Summary

The word *communication* means "to hold in common," "to impart or share." Common assumptions about communication in preaching are often in error. The communication process can be understood with a cybernetic model that includes *sender, receiver, message, channel, encoding, decoding, feedback, noise, context,* and *field of experience.* Rather than action or interaction, communication is best understood as transaction. In preaching the key element is the work of the Holy Spirit. Communication involves a number of different levels, including

71

intrapersonal, interpersonal, small-group, mass, intercultural, and *orga-nizational.*

Review Questions

1. What is the meaning of the Latin root for *communication?*
2. Explain the meaning of *oral* and *aural.*
3. Discuss some of the mistaken assumptions about speech communication.
4. Identify and explain ten factors involved in the communication process.
5. Explain the communication models represented by the words *action, interaction,* and *transaction.*
6. What is the role of the Holy Spirit as a factor in the communication process?
7. Explain the various levels of communication as to audience size and speaker-audience relationship.

CHAPTER FIVE

THE SOUND OF A VOICE

T he human voice is a marvelous instrument. You only have to listen to a trained singer to be impressed with the versatility, range, control, and expressiveness of the human voice. The most marvelous capability of man with his voice is that he can speak. He can manipulate the various elements that are involved in vocal production to produce sounds that carry his thoughts to others.

Scientists and philosophers have debated for centuries whether any other animal but man is capable of speech. Until recently the debate centered on language. It was thought that no animal had the ability to communicate in language, to put thoughts together and hold an intelligent conversation. Then, in the 1970s chimpanzees were taught to use sign language. Previous efforts to teach them to speak had failed. Their vocal apparatus was not capable of speech. So the debate shifted. While apes could apparently use language (sign language), only man could speak.

Every organ used in speech has another use biologically. The lungs, the tongue, teeth and lips, the vocal cords, and various resonators function in normal ways necessary to life. In the miracle of speech we conceptualize meanings, attach them to complex sounds we call words, and produce those sounds with such subtlety and variety that others not only understanding the concepts but also discern our attitude about them.

In everything we say we use three main languages. We use *word language* to carry the meaning we wish to communicate to others. We use *tone language* as the nonverbal emphasis and color our tone of voice carries. We also use *body language*, the various nonvocal and nonverbal signals we send to accompany our words. The voice carries two of these languages: the *words* we speak and the *tone* of voice. In the next chapter we will address the matter of nonverbal communication in more detail. For now, our aim is to understand how the voice is produced and what can be done to improve vocal production for speech.

Speech is produced in four stages: *breathing, phonation, resonation,* and *articulation.* Though these four phases overlap and function simultaneously, there is a basic sequence in speech production. First, the power for speech sounds comes in a column of air from the lungs. Second, the sound itself is produced by the vibration of the vocal folds. Third, the various resonators amplify the spoken sounds to project them to the hearer. Fourth, the tongue, teeth, and lips shape those sounds to produce words. We will look at vocal production in these four stages.

BREATHING FOR SPEECH

The main purpose for breathing is to bring oxygen into the body and carry away waste, especially carbon dioxide. Through the simple passage of air in and out of the lungs, this vital process takes place.

Inhalation begins with a signal from the brain which activates the *diaphragm*, and the muscles surrounding the ribs. The diaphragm is a membranous muscular partition between the chest cavity and the abdominal cavity. In the resting position, the diaphragm is arched upward like a dome. Inhalation takes place when it contracts, to lower and flatten while the rib cage expands. This draws air into the lungs from outside as the lower pressure inside the chest cavity creates a vacuum. Exhalation occurs when the diaphragm relaxes to its resting position like a dome while the rib cage settles down, thus forcing the air in the lungs out through the windpipe.

Breathing for speech differs from nonspeech breathing in that it is more controlled and deeper, with inhalation quicker and exhalation more sustained. Control of a good supply of air is the foundation for effective vocal production. In quiet inhalation you ordinarily use four sets of muscles, whereas in controlled exhalation for speech, you must use five to ten sets of muscles.[1] Just as your voice reveals much about your personality and attitude, it also reveals much about your physical condition. When a preacher gasps and wheezes like a drowning man, audience attention is drawn to his physical condition and distracted from his message.

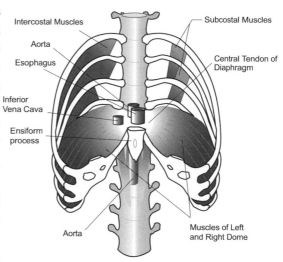

Intercostal Muscles

Aorta

Esophagus

Inferior Vena Cava

Ensiform process

Subcostal Muscles

Central Tendon of Diaphragm

Aorta

Muscles of Left and Right Dome

Nothing affects breathing like your posture. Breathing habits and posture are interrelated. Not only does posture affect the way you breath, but your breathing habits also affect your body balance, distribution of weight, relaxation, and appearance. Any physical activity, to be efficient and enjoyable, must be supported by good conditioning and good habit patterns in breathing. The beginning point for good breathing habits is good posture.

Posture for good breathing is often misunderstood. Bad habits of posture are common. You have seen a speaker or singer stand rigidly erect, chest out, shoulders high, muscles of the neck tense with veins standing out. This posture is not right for breathing. As you stand up and breathe deeply, you may find your abdominal wall moving in with inhalation, just the opposite of natural breathing. For a good example, notice how a sleeping baby breathes, his abdominal wall rising and falling as the diaphragm draws the air in and then expels it.

To practice effective breathing for speech and singing, think of filling up your entire abdominal and chest cavities with air. You fill your body from the bottom up, throwing the air down in a gushing stream that fills you up. Of course, this is not what is happening, but when you visualize inhalation this way, the sensation will lead to better breathing patterns.

Arthur Lessac, an expert in speech and voice therapy, based his speech method on the sense-memory of natural and correct breathing.[2]

If you can experience correct breathing and remember how it feels, you can develop the habit of correct breathing by recreating that same bodily sensation. Lessac held that correct breathing and posture are relatively easy to achieve. Even though very few people breathe correctly while standing up, no one can breathe incorrectly while bending over or lying on his back. In these positions (along with some others), the muscles "fall naturally into the relationships that lead to good posture and counteract faulty conditioning, allowing the body to breathe as it wants to breathe."[3]

Instead of attempting to stand correctly for good breathing, learn how it feels to breathe correctly and then do the same while you stand. In this method, your breathing will correct your posture and that correct posture will, in turn, allow for correct breathing. But remember that old habits do not give way easily. They can only be replaced by new habits. Major changes may be necessary in the way you stand. As you concentrate on reproducing the feel of correct breathing, your posture will begin to conform to the best position for that breathing.

"Correct breathing for speech is natural and almost effortless."

Correct breathing for speech is natural and almost effortless. When compared to the amount of air available, very little breath is necessary to vibrate the vocal cords, even for a forceful tone. Extra effort or strain in breathing only indicates you are trying to manipulate the flow of air unnaturally. As you speak, you must not concentrate on breathing. Your thought is on what your are saying and how you want to say it. "Remember that breath control does not regulate voice production—rather, voice production regulates breath control."[4]

Lessac suggests a number of exercises for natural breathing.[5] Two of the simplest are probably the most effective as well: breathing in the lying-down position and breathing in the sitting position. These exercises are designed to teach you to feel the natural breathing function. Once you know the physical sensation of natural breathing in these positions, you can recreate that same sensation while standing and thus take posture appropriate for natural breathing. In the two positions described below, you will automatically breathe in the natural and correct manner. You cannot breathe incorrectly in these positions.

For the first exercise, lie down on a firm mattress. Make yourself feel as light as possible, as though all your weight is being eliminated. Stretch your body to make it as long as possible, keeping your knees loose but not raised. Now you are comfortably relaxed and breathing naturally, with the body alignment you want to achieve when you are standing. Notice your breathing. Your abdominal muscles just below the rib cage swell out and go in. Your sides at the waistline also gently expand. Try to be as observant as possible and to sense just what is happening and how it feels—in your abdomen, your sides, your back.

After making a mental note of how this natural breathing feels, stand up and try to reproduce these same sensations as you breathe quietly. Look at your abdominal wall. If it moves inward instead of outward as you inhale, you can see that it is just the opposite of your correct breathing as you lie down. Do not be discouraged. Just lie down and repeat the exercise. Keep it up until you begin to reproduce the same sensations standing as you experience lying down. Remember, concentrate on how it feels and make it happen again.

> *"There is nothing more important for good vocal production than good breathing and posture, which are inseparable."*

A second exercise is in the sitting position. Sit on the edge of a chair, leaning forward with your elbows resting just above your knees, your hands hanging loosely between your knees and your feet comfortably flat on the floor. Breathe naturally and memorize the action-sensation. Inhale and exhale a number of times. Then hold your breath and stand, trying to retain the same feeling as you had sitting. Inhale and exhale a few times and check for the same breathing action you had in the sitting position.

Two aspects of your posture are key to sensing the correct alignment of your body for natural breathing. The first is the head position. Stand with the crown of your head as the highest part of the body, your chin level never raised, the back of your neck extended upward, and the front of the neck loose, and never stretched. A second important feature of good posture for natural breathing is to rock your pelvis forward, thus bringing the abdominal wall inward and upward.

There is nothing more important for good vocal production than good breathing and posture, which are inseparable. Though all of this may seem too complicated to remember, do not be discouraged. Try the exercises. Check your breathing to see whether it is the same standing as in the exercise position. If you see that you have bad breathing habits, continue the exercises. You may also want to seek out a voice teacher or speech therapist to help you develop new habits.

Phonation for Speech

The second stage of speech production is *phonation*, the producing of a sound. This sound is produced by the vibration of the vocal cords as air from the lungs pushes through. That very simple description, however, may leave you with the wrong impression as to what is taking place with phonation. The vocal "cords" are not cords, or strings at all. They are muscles of the larynx which actually serve as one of two valves designed to keep foreign material out of your windpipe and lungs.

The larynx, where the sound is produced, is a complicated structure. It is like a box with walls of cartilage lined with muscular tissues and membranes. It is attached by muscles on its outer surface to structures of the head and neck above and the chest below. This "box" sits at the top of the windpipe (trachea) and is open at the top and bottom to allow a flow of air from the lungs. This passageway

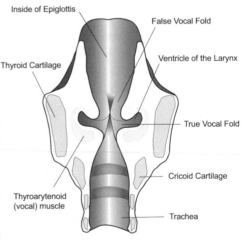

through the larynx is controlled by a double valve, with one part of this valve at the top and the other inside the box.[6]

This double valve system closes when you swallow to divert swallowed material to the esophagus and into the stomach. In the swallowing action, the entire structure of the larynx rises so that the valve tissue fits against a small leaf-shaped cartilage at the base of the tongue called the epiglottis. This seals off the trachea (windpipe) and sends swallowed material into the esophagus, which leads to the stomach. Occasionally the upper valve allows something to slip past, "down the wrong pipe," and triggers a cough to expel the offending matter. If something gets past the second valve (the true vocal folds), it goes into the windpipe and can cause suffocation.

The upper valve is called the "false vocal folds," which do not normally vibrate to produce sound. They do protect the true vocal folds, the lower valve. When the biological function of the larynx is considered, the speech function is all the more remarkable. The vocal folds are in reality the thyro-artenoid muscles. They project from the inner walls of the larynx as indicated in the drawing on page 78.

The vocal cords might better be called "voice lips" since they function much like the lips of a trumpet player. They are actually quite small, roughly three quarters of an inch long in men and a half inch in women.[7] The tone is produced by the vibration or flutter on the edges of the folds as they are drawn together and air is forced between them. The edges of the folds are wedge shaped and rather rounded, overlaid with a pearly white, tough, fibrous tissue. This shape and texture of the vocal folds make possible a rich, mellow sound for speech.[8]

The most common faults with vocal tone include *breathiness, hoarseness or huskiness, harshness and stridency, throatiness, absence of vibrato, juvenile voice, faulty pitch level*, and *faults of vocal intensity*.[9] Though some of these faults may be attributable to malformation, injury, or disease of the vocal folds, most probably stem from unfortunate speech habits. Some reflect childhood mimicking of adults. Others indicate personality problems. Still others may be caused by misuse and abuse of the voice. A speech pathologist or ear, nose, and throat specialist should be consulted for diagnosis and treatment.

Preachers are susceptible to various problems with their voices. Even a cold or sore throat can cause the membranes to become inflamed and swell, and mucus to collect in the throat and other passages. These conditions usually cause the voice to be husky, coarse, and lacking in nasal resonance. Though this may be only a temporary condition, there are other problems of a more permanent nature. Enlarged tonsils and adenoids can result in faulty tongue, jaw, and soft-palate positions and affect the voice. Other culprits are chronic nasal or throat infections related to asthma, infected sinuses, and allergies.[10]

The misuse of the voice by preachers is also the cause of chronic problems. Poor breath support can lead to tension in the throat in an effort to force a greater sound from a weak stream of air. You will see this in speakers and singers when the veins and ligaments of the throat stand out and that pinched quality is heard in the voice. Most of us can tell the difference between preaching loudly enough to be heard and abusing our voices. This strain can also lead to the development of nodules or polyps on the vocal folds.

"When breath support is poor, we tend to focus our energy on the throat in an effort to force a strong voice for speaking."

A preacher suffering from voice problems should take seriously symptoms such as hoarseness, throat pain, and swallowing problems. Even though other causes might be found, these symptoms are the warning signs of laryngeal cancer. Most voice disorders, however, are the result of misuse and abuse of the voice. Diagnosis and treatment of voice problems should involve a team approach, including both an ear, nose, and throat specialist (ENT) and a speech pathologist. An ENT evaluation will search out the physical causes and symptoms. A voice evaluation by a speech therapist will identify faulty speech habits which may be the root of the problem.

For the most part, a preacher should make sure his breathing is natural and adequate for public speech. The breathing exercises described above will help. When breath support is poor, we tend to focus our energy on the throat in an effort to force a strong voice for speaking. This causes tenseness in the throat, including the pharynx, which may cause hoarseness, pain, vocal nodules, and laryngitis, along with other problems. Your immediate aim as a preacher is to manage your voice carefully so as to avoid stress in your throat and jaw. As you speak, the tension should be in your abdominal muscles, with the throat area relaxed and loose.

Here is an initial exercise, to test whether there is excessive strain in your throat.[11] Place your finger in the notch of the thyroid cartilage, just at the top of the "Adam's apple." While you hold it there, speak in a loud, sharp tone as if to give a military order to men some distance away, "Ready! Aim! Fire!" If the thyroid cartilage (Adam's apple) rises very much while you say this, you are focusing too much tension in the throat instead of in the abdominal muscles. You will easily be able to tell if the thyroid cartilage disappears up under the hyoid bone at the base of the tongue as it does in swallowing.

This tension in the throat should be avoided because it results in a pinched voice, undue strain on the vocal folds, and the hoarseness which follows. Besides developing good breathing habits, you can practice relaxing your neck and jaw as you speak. Brigance suggests the following exercises as a start.[12] (1) Relax all muscles of the jaw and shake your head until the jaw flops. (2) Drop your head forward as if you were almost asleep. Then gradually begin shaking your head, using the muscles in the back of your neck. Increase the shaking until the jaw wobbles. (3) Yawn gently but thoroughly, and note at the finish how the muscles of the jaw and throat feel when relaxed. This is the muscle tone you want while speaking.

RESONATION FOR SPEECH

The third phase of vocal production is *resonation*. Though it has great potential, the initial sound produced by the vibration of the vocal folds is but a squeak—weak, poor in quality, and having little carrying power.[13] Think of a musical instrument and the difference resonation makes in its sound. If you strike a tuning fork, you will hear only a weak tone. If you set the base of it on a table, however, the sound will be amplified through the wood. A trumpet tone produced through the mouthpiece alone sounds like a weak duck call, but add the trumpet with its tubing and bell and you have an entirely different sound.

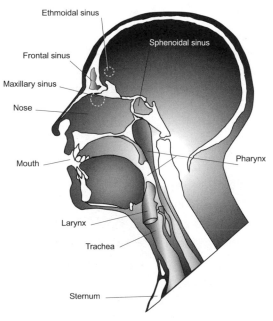

This amplification and enhancement of the sound is resonation. The human voice has a variety of res-

81

onators to enhance the sound. They are of two types: fixed and adjustable. *Fixed resonators* are those bones of the head and chest which serve as sounding boards for the voice. These include the skull bones, particularly the facial bones, the sternum (chest bone) and the ribs. *Adjustable resonators* are those that can be changed in size, shape, and tenseness. These are the mouth, the pharynx, and the larynx. With adjustments made in these resonators, you can change the pitch of your voice, giving it a rising and falling inflection, and make subtle variations in vocal quality, particularly with vowels.[14]

Sound may be analyzed and described by four basic characteristics: *time, pitch, loudness* (or intensity), and *quality* (or timbre).[15] The first factor, *time,* simply refers to the duration of the sound. While this characteristic is not a function of resonation, the other three are. Your adjustment of the vocal folds and resonators allow you to change the *pitch* of your voice. This is a most complex process, but it is controlled very naturally and easily in speaking and singing. *Loudness* is also determined largely by resonation, with adjustments in the force of phonation as well. The *quality* of the vocal tone is controlled by resonation, along with the shape, size, and condition of your vocal folds.

Poor resonation can be caused by tenseness which affects the texture of the resonators' surfaces. Stress in the throat and jaw as you speak will produce a more strident, harsher tone. Resonation is also hindered by the restriction of the area of adjustable resonators. Poor resonation is also caused by speech habits that misdirect the tone. *Hyponasality* refers to the muffled, cold-in-your-head sound when the nasal passage is blocked or restricted. *Hypernasality* is the whining sound of too much nasal resonation caused by misdirected tone.

One of the most common causes of poor resonation is the restriction of the full potential of the oral cavity. The mouth is the largest of the resonators, with some 25 percent of the total resonation capacity. The pharynx, that large area which connects the mouth and nasal passages, is next in size. These two areas provide almost half the total resonation area.[16] Unfortunately, most people underutilize the potential of the mouth to amplify and enhance the sound of the voice.

Arthur Lessac emphasizes the "muscular sensations and kinesthetic memory" in prescribing exercises for developing full resonance for the voice.[17] This method is based on the tendency of the muscles to return to familiar positions, and recreating the feeling or "action-sensation" of correct facial posture. In other words, if you can shape your oral cavity in the best way for good resonation, and remember the sensation of that position, you can reproduce that shape when you speak.

The feeling he recommends for good resonation is that of a mega- phone turned around inside the oral cavity. To sense this position, imagine a megaphone shape, with the wide end expanding the middle of your mouth cav- ity at the cheekbones, beneath the eyes, and the narrow end protruding and rounding the lips. If you open your mouth wide to say "AH" and slowly alter 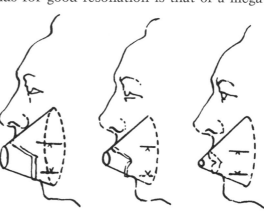 the sound until you get to the vowel "OO," you will probably feel the teeth closing with the lips. As a result, when you get to the smallest lip opening, the oral cavity is also greatly reduced. Lessac holds that the cavity size should be maintained throughout the pronunciation of these vowels.

As an experiment to check on the resonance of the oral cavity, open wide with the megaphone position.[18] Now place your two middle fin- gers against your cheek just behind the lips, separating your teeth. You may want to induce a comfortable yawn to check the opening. Now, begin with the "AH" sound and move gradually through "AW" and "OH" to "OO," without allowing the teeth to close. Using a tape recorder, pronounce these vowels first in your normal way. Then repeat the pronunciation using the megaphone position and keeping your teeth apart with the fingers. Now play back the recording and lis- ten for the difference in sound.

As in any change of habit, you will initially feel that the megaphone position is unnatural and probably looks strange. The feeling only tells you that your habitual way of talking is closing off much of the res- onation of the oral cavity. You may check the mirror for the look. Though those closest to you may notice the difference, it will not look odd. The "lazy jaw" habit can be overcome, even though you will initially feel that you are overworking your mouth in your speech.

Just as with breathing and phonation, resonation is a complex process. Problems with your voice quality and projection probably reflect bad habits developed since childhood. Do not think they will be easy to overcome. One of the best ways to practice with your voice is singing. You may want to become part of a choral group or take class voice lessons. While singing you can practice correct breathing, relaxed and natural phonation, and full resonation. The sustained tones will give you an opportunity to note the position and feel of your body as you reproduce the best postures for vocal production.

Articulation for Speech

The word *articulate* has two meanings: (1) segmented or formed in distinct units, as in a truck and trailer; and (2) joined or brought together in sequence, as in the clear expression of ideas. Both ideas are important for understanding articulation in speech. *Articulation* involves the production of distinct sound units and their combination into syllables, words, and phrases. A related word, *pronunciation*, has a broader meaning that can include articulation. *Pronunciation* has to do with the speech formation of words in a given language in the normally acceptable fashion.

At the average rate of speech, you say about five syllables a second. Your hearers must catch these sounds on the fly and translate them into thought. At that speed they have little time to hesitate or falter in their reception of the sounds. If your speech is slurred, muffled, or projected weakly, the hearer is under stress because he cannot go back and get what he missed. While he is trying to decipher what you just said, he can miss what you are saying now.

Articulation can be understood in terms of the various sound units we use in speech.[19] Even though we think of *words* as the main units of speech, they are not primarily significant phonetic units. In normal speech the *phrase* becomes the major unit which is spoken as a continuity of sound. In a strictly phonetic analysis, it would be

> "Articulation involves the production of distinct sound units, and their combination into syllables and phrases."

broken down directly into syllables, without much attention to the words, as such. Phrases are breath groups separated by pauses that make up normal speech. A phrase is spoken with continuous flow as each syllable merges into the next one.

Another unit of speech is the *syllable.* It is "a combination of sounds produced on a single impulse of breath power."[20] *Syllables* can be formed of almost any combination of sounds. The identifying mark of a syllable, as the definition above indicates, is that it is produced by a distinct impulse of voice or breath. The center of a syllable is usually a vowel or diphthong, which provides the most fully vocalized sound of the unit. Consonants provide the boundaries of syllables, and, at the same time, link syllables together as phrases.

The yet smaller units of speech are the *phonemes*, which are the individual speech sounds that make up syllables. The distinct and constant sound of a vowel or consonant will vary because of the influence of adjacent sounds. The sound of "t" in top, pot, and button is a phoneme that is identifiable but varies with different usages. Due to this tendency of phonemes to adapt to the sound context, this basic unit is not so much a particular sound as a family of sounds which are alike enough to be identified as the same yet may vary with usage.

Sound units, the *phonemes*, of a particular language will vary, depending on how discriminating the person doing the counting. The number of sound units in English is 40 to 45, while our alphabet has only 26 letters. It is very difficult to represent these various sounds with written symbols. Dictionaries use various markings and still offer six or eight sounds represented by the single letter "a."

In English the problem is complicated by the fact that our spelling is not phonetic. In fact, the English language is the most interesting in the world when it comes to variations in pronunciation of the same apparent spelling. An anonymous poet has captured the confusion.[21]

> When the English tongue we speak,
> Why is *break* not rhymed with *freak*?
> Will you tell me why it's true
> We say *sew*, but likewise *few*?
> And the maker of the verse
> Cannot cap his *horse* with *worse*?
> *Beard* sounds not the same as *heard*;

Cord is different from *word*;
Cow is cow, but *low* is low;
Shoe is never rhymed with *foe*.
Think of *hose* and *dose* and *lose*,
And of *goose* and yet of *choose*.
Think of *comb* and *tomb* and *bomb*.
Doll and *roll*, and *home* and *some*,
And since *pay* is rhymed with *say*
Why not *paid* with *said*, I pray?
We have *blood* and *food* and *good*;
Mould is not pronounced like *could*.
Wherefore *done*, but *gone*, and *lone*?
Is there any reason known?
And, in short, it seems to me
Sounds and letters disagree.

Dealing with the problem of spelling and pronunciation can be difficult in any language. One solution is provided by the International Phonetic Alphabet. The IPA uses characters and symbols to indicate the basic units of sound, the *phonemes*. Regardless of the variations in spelling, only one symbol in the IPA is used for each sound. This allows much more precise guidance than the system used in dictionaries for the pronunciation of a word. Once you learn the IPA, it is simple to use. Learning it, however, is beyond the scope of this study.

Even with the difficulty of pronunciation in English, the normal audience will expect a preacher to speak clearly and correctly. Mispronunciation and misarticulation can distract from the message and damage the credibility of the preacher. Most errors of articulation are the result of simple laziness. Speech teachers often admonish students about *lazy lips* and *lazy jaw*. Even though the idea and the word are clearly in mind, when you say it the result is not clear. In a hurry to express yourself, you may fall into the habit of mumbling, slurring, and abbreviating.

Mispronunciation can also be caused by ignorance. We learn to speak by copying those around us. When their speech is not precise and correct (as it seldom is in casual conversation) we fall into those same patterns. In public speech, however, articulation and pronunciation must be more careful, and even exaggerated, in order to be understood by the mass audience. Remember that you must speak with an enlarged style in order to reach the person farthest from you.

Mispronunciations fall into four categories: sounds *added*, sounds *omitted*, and sounds *substituted*, plus wrong *accent*. Sounds can be added, like saying "flusterated" for "flustered," or pronouncing the "t" in "often." Sounds can be omitted, like saying "reglur" for "regular" or "Florda" for "Florida." Sounds can be substituted, like saying "jist" for "just" or "thang" for "thing." Words can be pronounced with the wrong accent, like saying "POH-lees" for "police" or "DEE-troit" for "Detroit."

Some words are mispronounced in several ways at once. Take as an example the word "electricity," which I have heard pronounced "lek-TRIS-tee." How would you describe the errors in this pronunciation? How about the pronunciation "HUN-ert" for the word "hundred?" What mistakes are involved? What happens to *genuine* when it is pronounced "JIN-yu-WINE?"

Here are some words to watch in your pronunciation. These are often mispronounced. Identify the kind of error involved for each word and pronounce the word correctly.[22]

rapport	ruh-PORE, not ra-PORT
subtle	SUH-tul, not SUB-tul
often	OFF-un, not OFF-tun
err	UR, not AIR
toward	TORD, not tuh-WARD
escape	es-CAYP, not eks-CAYP
nuclear	NEW-klee-ur, not NEWK-yuh-lur
realtor	REEL-tur, not RE-luh-tur
Cuba	KYOO-buh, not KYOO-ber
adult	uh-DULT, not ADD-ult
larynx	LAIR-inks, not LAR-nix
cavalry	CAV-ul-ree, not CAL-vuh-ree
jewelry	JEW-ul-ree, not JEW-ler-ee
candidate	CAN-duh-date, not CAN-uh-date
library	LI-brer-ee, not LI-bair-ee
picture	PICK-chur, not PIH-chur
relevant	RELL-uh-vant, not REV-uh-lunt

Especially important for the preacher is the pronunciation of biblical names and places and words related to ministry. Notice the sound of the following words:

Jerusalem	Juh-ROO-su-lem, not DROOS-luhm
Nehemiah	NEE-uh-MIGH-uh, not nee-MIRE
Israel	IZ-rih-ul, not IZ-ruhl
Abednego	uh-BED-ne-go, not uh-BIN-dee-go
Nebuchadnezzar	NEB-yu-kud-NEZ-ur, not NEB-uh-NEZ-ur
pastoral	PAS-tu-rul, not pas-TOH-rul
funeral	FYOO-ner-ul, not FYOON-rul
children	CHIL-dren, not CHUL-drin or CHIL-ern
piano	pee-AN-oh, not pee-AN-er
secretary	SEK-ru-TAIR-ee, not SEK-ur-TAIR-ee

Many of these erroneous pronunciations may be part of the normal speech in the preacher's background. He may need to become bilingual, adding a more standard American English to his "down home" dialect.

The sound of the human voice is a marvelous thing. It is a miracle of God that He has given speech to man, of all His creation. In this sense, as in many others, we are made in His image. He is the God who speaks, and we are to speak too. How we speak is so important to our preaching that it can become an overwhelming factor that obscures and detracts from our message. On the other hand, the way you use your voice can so enhance your message as to make the difference in whether it is received.

But the voice is not your only means of communication in preaching. In the next chapter we will see that preaching is "more than words" as we examine the challenge and power of nonverbal communication.

Chapter Summary

Speech is a wonderful gift of God to man. Speech production is in four stages: *breathing, phonation, resonation,* and *articulation.* Control of a good supply of air is the foundation for effective vocal production. Breathing is affected by posture, physical conditioning, and breathing habits. Improvement in breathing can be attained by the use of exercises which allow natural breathing.

Phonation is the producing of a sound and takes place in the *larynx*, or voice box, with the vibration of the vocal folds. Phonation is best with good breath support and relaxation of the throat area.

Resonation is the amplification and enhancement of the sound. Full resonation requires relaxed muscles of the throat and face, openness in the adjustable resonators, and correct direction of the tone.

Articulation involves the production of distinct sound units and their combination into syllables, words, and phrases. Misarticulation and mispronunciation are usually caused by laziness or ignorance. The correctness and clarity of a preacher's speech may determine whether it is received.

REVIEW QUESTIONS

1. Identify the four stages of vocal production.
2. What is the *diaphragm* and how does it function in breathing?
3. Explain Arthur Lessac's approach to voice training.
4. How does posture affect breathing for speech?
5. What is the *larynx* and how does it function in speech?
6. What are the common voice problems preachers experience?
7. What is *resonation* and how does it work in speech?
8. Define *articulation* and its part in speech.
9. In what ways are words commonly mispronounced?

CHAPTER SIX

MORE THAN WORDS

As preachers, we tend to concentrate on the words of the messages we are presenting. Sometimes we labor over those words, working to craft just the right statement of sermon ideas or the clever turn of a phrase. That's what preaching is. Words. One word after another until a message is presented to the audience.

There are other channels of communication in preaching besides the words you say. When you are preaching face to face with your hearers, they are receiving 65 percent of your message by means other than words. Your audience is getting a number of messages from you at the same time. Amazing as it is, only 35 percent of speech communication may be verbal. These other channels for communication are tone of voice, facial expressions, gestures, even the way you stand and how you are dressed.[1]

So preaching is much more than words. The verbal message is accompanied by nonverbal messages that signal your attitudes, your personality, your character, your background, your relationship with the audience, and much more. *Nonverbal* means "without words." We have noted that *oral* means "by mouth" and has come to be used for spoken communication. *Verbal* means "by use of words," whether spoken or written. *Nonverbal*, then, is the

> *"The audience will probably judge the effectiveness of your preaching more by nonverbal elements than verbal."*

91

way we designate all the human communication channels that do not use words to carry the message.

The audience will probably judge the effectiveness of your preaching more by nonverbal elements than verbal. Allen H. Monroe found that audience members think of effective public speaking more in terms of delivery than content.[2] In a study of student responses to speeches, he discovered that the first six characteristics they associated with an ineffective speaker were related to delivery.

The most distracting feature of delivery named by Monroe's students was a monotonous voice. Others were stiffness, lack of eye contact, fidgeting, lack of enthusiasm, and a weak voice. The student audience liked direct eye contact, alertness, enthusiasm, a pleasant voice, and physical movement. Another student study discovered that for persuasive speeches, delivery was almost three times as important for effectiveness as content.[3]

Whether you or your hearers are conscious of these nonverbal factors, they are having their impact. Just by being there you are communicating, without saying a word. In fact, you cannot *not* communicate. David Hesselgrave writes, "It seems we cannot do *anything* without communicating *something*. To stand is to stand somewhere. And both the "standing" and the "somewhere" communicate."[4] The nonverbal elements are constantly sending out signals about who you are, your attitudes, your intentions, your sincerity. And these signals are believed. They affect your relationship with your audience before you even begin to speak.

We very often do not handle our nonverbal communication well. We send signals we do not intend and do not even know we are sending them. Others form opinions about us from our nonverbal communication. Common stereotypes demonstrate the conclusions we come to on the basis of nonverbal signals:[5] *A person who doesn't maintain direct eye contact isn't being sincere. If you're not looking at me, you are not interested in what I am saying. A person who dresses poorly cannot be trusted. Men with high-pitched voices are effeminate. Men with low-pitched voices are more credible than those with high-pitched voices. A person sitting with arms folded across the chest is being closed or defensive. Crying is a sign of weakness.*

Though few of us would agree to all of these stereotypes, we find our opinions of others affected by just such signals. Since nonverbal elements in speech are not easily isolated, the hearer does not really analyze why he feels the way he does about the speaker. He just gets an overall impression by all the signals he is receiving. It is the harmony of many factors that makes the message clear. Pearson and Nelson cite research indicating that most misunderstandings in oral communication can be traced to the nonverbal signals.[6]

"Our personality and attitudes may carry so much weight in the thinking of the audience that our words are overwhelmed."

The serious study of nonverbal communication is a fairly recent development. Though some writers have traced the discipline back to Greek rhetoric, others see the first serious mention of it in the nineteenth century efforts to catalog gestures and body movements.[7] Even though scholars still disagree about definitions and the meaning of the messages we send nonverbally, now there is a large and growing body of research and theory about nonverbal communication.

What does such research mean to a preacher? At least it indicates that we cannot separate the message from the messenger. Our personality and attitudes may carry so much weight in the thinking of the audience that our words are overwhelmed. In this chapter we will survey the various kinds of nonverbal communication. Then we will look at how nonverbal signals relate to the words we use. Finally, we will outline some of the principles by which we can understand and improve nonverbal communication.

Your nonverbal communication includes your bodily movements, gestures, and facial expressions. Other nonverbal signals, called *paralanguage*, are related to the use of your voice, such as variety, rate, pitch, and tone of voice. A third set of nonverbal signals come from external factors such as your clothing and your use of space and time.

BODILY MOVEMENTS

Kinesics is the study of bodily movements. The word comes from the Greek word *kenesis*, meaning motion or movement. These nonverbal channels include posture, gestures, and facial expressions. Your bodily movements will communicate to your audience your feelings and attitudes about your subject, about the audience, and about yourself. Some of these signals are obvious, and the hearer knows he is perceiving them. Others are *subliminal*, received by the audience at a subconscious level. The various levels of sophistication of your audience will determine how much they "read" of your body language.

Basic to body movement as such is body type and shape. You will inevitably be affected in your movements by how tall you are, your weight, physical conditioning, and health. Though it is a sensitive issue, physical condition, especially weight, will affect the attitude of your audience toward you before you say a word. An obviously overweight young preacher was told by his brother that he really had nothing to say about discipline and self-control. His own size destroyed his credibility. Considering how important these themes are to the Christian message, the young preacher recognized that his weight would keep him from an effective ministry.

> *"Those in an audience who cannot see the speaker clearly do not grasp his message as well as those who can."*

Even when your hearers do not actually think about your bodily movements and what they are saying, the signals are being received nonetheless. They may say, if only to themselves, *That visiting preacher seemed a bit arrogant and uppity to me.* Or they may think, *I really like this man; he is so sincere and genuine.* Research has demonstrated that those in an audience who cannot see the speaker clearly do not grasp his message as well as those who can.[8] The process of seeing signals, interpreting their meaning, and formulating an appropriate response is continuous as long as a person can see you.

In the area of bodily movement, the preacher will be particularly concerned with platform movement, facial expressions, eye contact, and gestures.

Platform Movement. In the overall sense, your movement as you preach begins as you walk to the pulpit. Your posture will announce something about your own self-image, about your attitude, about your energy and vitality. If you slouch and stroll, you may be telling the people you are rather laid back and casual, an easygoing person ready to have a little chat with them. If, on the other hand, you jump up and stride quickly and energetically to the pulpit, you will signal the audience that you are forceful, here on serious business, and eager to get on with the message.

Depending on the audience, there may be significant differences of opinion about the preacher's movement on the platform as he preaches. In some churches the tradition is for the preacher to stay behind the pulpit and avoid unnecessary movement. In other churches there is no pulpit to use, and the preacher ordinarily moves about freely. Since body language is such an important part of the overall message, the best situation for communication would be to do without a pulpit altogether. In most cases, however, the preacher will be in a more traditional auditorium with a pulpit.

The problem with pulpits is not a new one. Henry Ward Beecher offered this rather vivid assessment more than a hundred years ago:

> You put a man in one of those barreled pulpits, where there is no responsibility laid upon him as to his body, and he falls into all manner of gawky attitudes, and rests himself like a country horse at a hitching post. He sags down, and has no consciousness of his awkwardness. But bring him out on a platform, and see how much more manly be becomes, how much more force comes out. The moment a man is brought face to face with other men, then does the influence of each act and react upon the other.[9]

Since you will usually speak from a pulpit, most of your body will be hidden from the audience. If you are short of stature, they may see little more than your head. If you are tall, you may tend to hunch over the pulpit as Beecher so vividly described. Either way the pulpit seems to be a barrier to good communication rather than a help.

Not only does local tradition and the physical arrangement of the platform suggest what movement is appropriate, but there is also a wide difference in what various preachers prefer. Platform movement is a reflection of a preacher's style. His personality is expressed in the way he moves. There are, however, some guidelines for movement that will apply to all preachers.

My first suggestion to you about platform movement is to *be aware of what your posture communicates*. Poor posture, slumped shoulders, and a generally slouched look suggest that you are lazy, lacking in con-

---

Platform Movement Guidelines

1. Be aware of what your posture communicates about character and attitude.
2. Start by establishing "home base" at the pulpit or center of the platform.
3. Move away from the center position only to emphasize a change of thought.

---

fidence, maybe even undisciplined. Posture is also important to your breathing and the effect that has on your speaking voice. Practice standing tall but not rigid. Consider whether your posture reflects the need for physical exercise and conditioning.

As you begin the sermon, *establish "home base" at the pulpit or at the center of the platform*. This is "center stage" in drama terms and is the strongest position on the platform. Once you have established this base at the pulpit, all platform movement will have the pulpit as its reference point. I have seen preachers begin their sermons away from the pulpit. This suggests to the audience that their comments are somewhat unofficial, that the sermon is not really starting yet. Beginning at the pulpit says that the sermon has begun and that the Word of God is being honored.

The long tradition behind the pulpit gives it a special place in the minds of believers. For those out of traditional church backgrounds, the pulpit represents the authority of God and His word. It is the official position for the Word of God to be declared. It is the "sacred desk" for such proclamation, and any other location is not quite as official or authoritative. This is why the removal of the pulpit from the platform usually stirs up a major controversy in a traditional church.

Once "home base" is established at the pulpit or platform center, *any movement away from that position should be connected with a change in sermon material*. Moving to the side of the pulpit suggests a more personal and intimate word is to be shared. You may want to move when you begin an illustration. You may also move to the side when you want to step closer to the audience and bring the biblical truth home with specific applications.

Very simply, platform movement should be purposeful. Avoid wandering around like a tiger pacing in a cage. This is an indication of restlessness or nervousness or may suggest a lack of experience preaching. I realize that some of us think better on our feet and think best when on the move. But remember that your movement is communicating something to your audience. Restless wandering can be a serious distraction that keeps your audience from concentrating on the message.

Gestures. In normal conversation we use our hands to augment our words. You have heard it said of an especially lively person that she cannot talk without her hands. Keeping her hands still is like wearing a gag. In everyday communication we do not think about these gestures. They are natural, unconscious, and spontaneous. A person who is animated in conversation may suddenly become aware of his hands when making a speech, not quite sure what to do with them. Then gestures may become unnatural and awkward.

Awkwardness in gestures can be a serious distraction to the audience. Steven and Susan Beebe have cataloged some of these awkward and unnatural gestures.[10] Sometimes uneasy speakers will grasp the lectern until their knuckles turn white. They may let their hands just flop around with no apparent purpose. One hand on a hip is the "broken wing" pose, only made worse with both hands on hips in the "double broken wing." A speaker may clutch one arm as though he has been grazed by a bullet. Hands in pockets may suggest relaxation in conversation but are usually not appropriate in preaching. Another unnatural gesture is to grasp one hand with the other and let them drop in front of you in a kind of "fig leaf clutch."

In public speech gestures are to function the same way they do in conversation. A conversational style of public address is the most natural and effective for preaching. We use gestures to emphasize important points, to point out places, to enumerate items, and to describe objects. In our preaching gestures work the same way. They augment what we are saying, underline it, clarify it, dramatize it, even communicate without words at all.

"Rather than practicing good gestures, try to eliminate distracting ones."

When a large pulpit hides the preacher from view, his gestures will be unnatural and awkward. Spurgeon gave a long and humorous complaint against pulpits as he lectured on gestures. Like Beecher, he saw them as a great hindrance to effective public speech, one no attorney in court would accept. "No barrister would ever enter a pulpit to plead a case at the bar," he said. "How could he hope to succeed while buried alive almost up to his shoulders? The client would be ruined if the advocate were thus imprisoned."[11] So will a pulpit often "bury" you and hinder your gestures.

Gestures function in six ways in relation to your speech:[12] (1)*repeating*, when gestures reinforce visually what you are saying, as in holding up three fingers while talking about three points; (2)*contradicting*, when gestures are in conflict with what you say; (3)*substituting*, when your hands speak without a word being said; (4)*complementing*, when gestures add further meaning to what is said; (5)*emphasizing*, when gestures support what you are saying by giving it force; (6)*regulating*, when gestures are used to control your interaction with the audience.

When you see yourself on videotape, you may notice that your gestures need to be improved. Keep these guidelines in mind. Effective gestures will be natural and relaxed. They will be definite and well-timed rather than uncertain. Also, work to make your gestures appropriate to what you are saying and, at the same time, adapted to the audience. Try to use variety and avoid overusing certain movements. Also, avoid gestures that call attention to themselves. Your aim is to have the audience focus on your message and not on your gestures.

Spurgeon focused on the critical issue when he told his students, "It is not so much incumbent upon you to acquire right pulpit action as it is to get rid of that which is wrong."[13] Rather than practicing good gestures, try to eliminate distracting ones. Spurgeons pointed out that "little oddities and absurdities" in gestures will prejudice the minds of the general public and detract from the message. He said that posture and gestures are the dress of the sermon. Just as no one would wear shabby clothes if he could get finer ones, so should the preacher clothe his message in the best dress he can.

Facial Expressions. Whereas gestures can augment our words with support for the ideas we are communicating, facial expressions primarily com-

"Facial expressions tell others how we feel, while body orientation tells them how intensely we feel it."

98

municate emotion. I have noticed that one of the most common criticisms mentioned in evaluating student preachers is that facial expression is weak, even "deadpan." When a preacher is talking about a life-changing matter and yet his face is lifeless, which do you think the audience will believe? Will they think his message is urgent when his face communicates indifference?

Part of our problem as preachers is that our facial expressions are not what we think they are. From inside we feel that our faces are expressive and animated. But the audience cannot see it. Try this. Put on what you feel is a normal and sincere smile. Then hold that expression while you turn to look in the mirror. You may well find that what you think you are expressing never quite gets to your face. You may have to practice facial expressions in the mirror where you can see what the audience sees. With some effort you can make whatever adjustments are needed for your face to express what you intend.

Managing facial expressions is very difficult. That is one reason for the high level of credibility given to facial expressions. They are naturally much more spontaneous and truthful than other body language. Researchers have discovered that facial expressions tell others how we feel, while body orientation tells them how intensely we feel it.[14] The message in facial expressions is not so much cognitive as emotional. They reinforce your message by revealing how you really feel about it.

It is difficult to mask what we really feel because our faces give us away. This brings us again to the difficulty of separating the message from the messenger in preaching. Your own feelings about the message you are delivering will so color the hearer's perception of it that he will likely accept it or reject it based on your attitude toward it. As much as any other kind of nonverbal communication, your facial expressions signal those feelings and attitudes. If your facial expressions and tone of voice do not communicate that the message is important, it must not be.

Eye Contact. The channel of body language that has the most impact on the hearer is eye contact. It is the eyes that tell you whether another person has noticed you and what his intentions are toward you. Eye contact tells you at once that you are the object of attention. Eyes indicate a person's mood more reliably than any other facial features. Eye signals are unselfconscious, genuine and hard to fake. We can tell from the eyes alone whether a person is pleased, wary, wistful or bored.[15]

The primary function of eye contact is to establish and define relationships with others. Close friends and family members can communicate with little more than a glance. When fellowship is broken, one of the first indications is the lack of eye contact. Resentment toward an acquaintance will be almost instantly perceived by the change in eye contact. Though we are hardly conscious of what is going on, reliable messages are being sent and received. The preacher's method of delivery should make allowance for maximum eye contact from the outset.

The preacher's eye contact with his audience serves several important functions.[16] It *opens communication, establishes rapport, checks on audience reactions, makes you more believable, expresses emotion,* and *keeps your audience interested.* Of all the nonverbal channels we are discussing, none of them is more important than eye contact.

First, eye contact *opens communication.* When you establish eye contact with a person, it is the equivalent of ringing her up on the phone. Eye contact other than a passing glance tells another that you are interested in talking. When the preacher comes to the pulpit and looks at his audience, he is opening that line of communication.

Eye contact in preaching, more than any other factor, *establishes rapport* with the audience, the compatibility and harmony that is necessary to persuasive speech. We trust people more when they look us in the eye. If there is a lack of eye contact, the audience feels they are not really in fellowship with the preacher. They tend to become restless and resistant to his message. Eye contact that reveals hostility is also quickly perceived by the audience and puts them in a defensive and resentful mode.

> *"The preacher's method of delivery should make allowance for maximum eye contact."*

Eye contact allows the preacher to *check on audience reactions* to his sermon. The best method of gauging the attention and interest of the audience is by reading facial expression, particularly the eyes. If his hearers look at him intently, the preacher knows they are with him and following his thoughts with interest. If they begin to avert their eyes by looking down or to the side, he knows they are disengaging. They are disconnecting the communication link and moving away. These signals allow the preacher to adapt his sermon to audience interest.

Eye contact with your audience *makes you believable*. The credibility issue is very important to the preacher. Studies have documented the connection between eye contact and increased credibility. Unless you maintain at least 50 percent eye contact with your audience, they will likely consider you unfriendly, uninformed, inexperienced, and even dishonest.[17]

> *"They give you their attention ... because your eye contact indicates your interest in them."*

Eye contact also serves to *display emotion*. Research has concluded that eye signals reveal emotion as much as any aspect of nonverbal communication. Some feel that the eyes alone reveal one's inner feelings. For the most part, however, the eyes can be the focus of attention for understanding the mood of another, with the face as the backdrop and reinforcer for eye signals. Since the preacher's attitude toward his subject and his audience are critical for getting his message across, it is vital that he maintain eye contact with his audience.

Eye contact helps to *keep the audience's interest*. When a speaker fastens his eyes on his manuscript or notes, that diversion immediately takes its toll on audience interest. When you are looking at your hearers, they are more likely to pay attention to you because that is the normal pattern in conversation. They give you their attention because your eye contact indicates your interest in them. As they read your passion for your subject in your eyes, they will be motivated to take it seriously.

Remember that eye contact has different meanings in different cultures. In Japan, for instance, the direct eye contact of American communication is seen as intrusive and aggressive. Even in the United States, the preacher will want to avoid fastening his gaze on individuals for too long or concentrating his attention in one area of the auditorium. Avoid rhythmic sweeps of the eyes from one side to the other without really seeing anyone. It is best to look at all areas of the audience and make brief eye contact with as many individuals as possible.

Body language is not just a side issue in preaching. The preacher's interest must go beyond the avoidance of distractions. Body language is a separate dialect, a broadcast band that can either reinforce your verbal message, neutralize it, or even negate it.

Nonverbal communication not only involves body language, but it also includes how you use your voice.

SIGNALS WITH YOUR VOICE

As we have already noted in chapter 5, voice problems can have any number of causes, from organic disorders to functional disorders. Our concern here, however, is with the sound and use of the voice as it communicates nonverbally. This area of study is closely related to the physiology of vocal production and to communication style.

The nonverbal channels in the quality of your voice and articulation are called *paralanguage*. Like other aspects of nonverbal communication, the way you use your voice in speech is directly tied to your whole personality. Personality affects your voice, and voice improvement can affect your personality. Remember the difference speech training made for Eliza Doolittle in *My Fair Lady*. Raymond Ross quotes an expert in voice and diction training, "Bluntly speaking, one may have a dull, uninteresting, or unpleasant voice because his voice is defective or improperly used; but he may also have such a voice because he is a dull, uninteresting, or unpleasant person."[18]

As in every other channel of nonverbal communication, the preacher's personality and character will come out, whether he intends it or not. Voice quality and language use can suggest to an audience that the preacher is forceful or lethargic, educated or ignorant, confident or fearful, pessimistic or optimistic, sincere or deceitful. As much as any other factor, people use the sound of your voice and your pronunciation to assess your level of competence and intellectual ability.

I am always amazed when deceitful and immoral preachers are exposed to the surprise of their congregations. I wonder how they could have carried on for so long without their hearers becoming suspicious. Nonverbal communication is very difficult to fake. After learning the truth about phony ministers, you will inevitably hear members of the congregation confess that they had been suspicious for some time but said nothing about it. They really wanted to believe in their pastor, so much so that they disregarded their own reading of the nonverbal messages.

Your voice is one of the most important factors affecting your image in the minds of others. The way they "see" you is constructed by what they hear. As soon as you begin to speak, your spoken image becomes dominant and overrides your visual image. When you talk, you are either reinforcing or destroying the message you are sending by gestures, facial expressions, clothing, posture and other non-verbal channels.[19] I remember a number of occasions when an immaculately dressed, well-groomed handsome person would present an impressive image, until he opened his mouth with a nasal, grammatically incorrect, and "backwoods" way of speaking.

> *"Your voice is one of the most important factors affecting your image in the minds of others."*

Simply enough, it is not only what you say but how you say it that is important. How you speak will be the major factor in whether people want to listen to you and take your ideas seriously. This may not seem fair, but it is nonetheless true. Though we can cite powerful, Spirit-filled preachers like D. L. Moody as exceptions to the rule, we are unwise to presume upon our audiences and the importance of our message by neglecting to take voice and diction seriously.

Important variables in your way of speaking include voice quality, speaking rate, volume, pitch, and melody. The key to effective use of these vocal qualities is variety. It is sameness and monotony in these areas that cause the hearer to lose interest. On the other hand, extremes in these areas can be out of place, even with variety. Other factors have to do with your use of language—articulation, pronunciation, and grammar. An audience is continually assessing these factors as to whether they sound like normal and acceptable speech.

Vocal variables will be discussed further in chapter 7 as we explore preaching style. Now let's consider some nonverbal channels that are external but communicate nonetheless.

External Factors

"You never get a second chance to make a first impression." That familiar quip carries a lot of common sense. Making a good impression is important to all of us. It is especially important to a preacher who wants his audience to respond positively to him and his message. He may be tempted to think that outward appearance is more important than personal sincerity. But showiness creates an image of artificiality and vanity. The preacher is wisest who is sensitive to his hearers and their expectations for one in his position. This is another aspect of the adaptation necessary to the speaker.

Clothes and Grooming. People will judge you by your *clothes and grooming*. The significance of clothing and other objects for communication is called *objectics*. Clothes give us protection from cold and rain, and they allow us modesty. But they also transmit messages about the wearer's personality, attitudes, social status, behavior, and group allegiances. While some of us are more sensitive to clothing than others, we all automatically take clothing into account when forming first impressions.

This outward appearance sends a message to others about your orderliness, taste, personal hygiene, sophistication, and other qualities. Some of the signals of sloppiness and lack of discipline are shoes not shined, tie crooked, rumpled clothing, mismatched colors and weaves, hair poorly combed or needing trimming, clothes too tight or too loose. Odor of breath and clothing also signal who you are and your sensitivity to others.

> *"Congregations expect their ministers to dress neatly, conservatively, and in good taste."*

In a seminar for business executives, a simple guideline for dress was offered that may also apply to preachers. Find out what the audience will be wearing, and wear clothes that are a trifle dressier than theirs. In dressing this way you set yourself off as the speaker and show your audience that you take their invitation seriously enough to dress up for them. At the same time, you do not overdress so that they can identify with you as someone enough like them to understand them.[20]

Style in dress for the preacher depends somewhat on local expectations. Some church traditions favor clerical robes. Like any uniform, a clerical robe downplays the personal element in favor of the position. As a general rule, congregations expect their ministers to dress neatly, conservatively, and in good taste. Though appropriate dress can vary from place to place, the preacher will not find it difficult to discover what local attitudes require.

Objectics can include any object that is commonly enough connected with you to reflect who you are. Beyond clothing, jewelry, watches, and other accessories, you may communicate more than you know by the car you drive. In one sense, a car is an extension of the need for clothing. Your car tells on you, your values, your priorities, your interests. Your house also communicates by the style of it, the size, the decorating, and the neighborhood.

Though not technically a part of your dress, what you have in your mouth is also a part of objectics. You know what a cigarette or pipe does to affect your impression of another. Though you probably do not smoke, let me suggest also that you never chew gum in public. Gum chewing has a high communicative value in signaling coarseness, ignorance, and indifference.

It is obvious in this brief look at *objectics* that every physical thing that is personally associated with you communicates a message about you. Even the little things that seem not to matter are sending their messages. As the familiar quip has it, "The devil is in the details."

Space, Touch, and Time. Another external factor that communicates nonverbally is your use of space. The study of the human use of space, called *proxemics*, was introduced by Edward T. Hall in a 1966 book.[21] He pointed to two important concepts on the use of space, *territoriality* and *personal space*. Territoriality refers to our need to establish and maintain certain spaces as our own. Personal space is the "personal bubble of space that moves around with you."[22]

Personal space is the distance you maintain between yourself and other people. It is the amount of space you claim as your own in your normal, everyday interaction with others. Hall identified four distances at which people commonly relate to others.[23] At the closest is *intimate distance*, out to about eighteen inches, which is used with people closest to us to show affection and comfort. Next is *personal distance*, from eighteen inches to four feet, the normal space Americans prefer for conversation. Third is *social distance*, from four to twelve feet, usually used for conducting business in the workplace. Finally, *public distance* is used most often in public speaking situations and runs from twelve feet and beyond.

Though the preacher will most often deliver his sermons at the *public* distance, how he relates at other levels will communicate his attitudes toward himself and others. You can be sure that the people are receiving multiple nonverbal messages even while you greet them before a service. If you draw too close to others in normal conversation, they may take it as an intrusion and see you as aggressive and insensitive. If you draw away, they may think you cold and unfriendly. Notice in the local situation how the people relate to one another. You can be sure they are noticing your use of personal space.

> *"You can be sure that the people are receiving multiple nonverbal messages even while you greet them before a service."*

Closely related to the use of space, though technically not an external factor, is *tactile communication*, the study of human touch. Since touch always invades another's space, it cannot be ignored. There are unspoken understandings as to what is appropriate and what is not in touch between adults. The preacher is wise to be careful about how much touching and hugging he does with his parishioners. Not only must he be sensitive to what is comfortable to others, but he must also realize that observers notice this behavior and see meaning in it.

Appropriate space and touch are both determined by cultural customs. Americans traveling abroad usually discover that Arabs, Latin Americans, and Southern Europeans are comfortable with much less personal space in their communication. In conversation they seem to stand too close. But when this makes Americans uncomfortable so that they step back, they may be seen as cold and rejecting by those of the other cultures. Touching is also culturally conditioned. Sidney Jourard discovered that the average touching in an hour of couples observed in public restaurants varied significantly from place to place: in San Juan, Puerto Rico 180 times; in Paris 110 times; in Gainesville, Florida twice, and in London, none at all.[24]

Touching and embracing are sensitive areas for a minister, calling for caution and alertness. On the one hand he wants to allow no impression that he is overly familiar, especially with women and girls. But he also wants to be able to express affection for his people. In some churches the custom involves hugging and other affectionate patting. In others this is not the custom. In one sense the minister should let his people set the pace according to their custom. On the other hand, he realizes that they may be waiting on him. This will result in a sort of getting acquainted dance until the question is settled satisfactorily.

No less than *space* and *touch*, your attitude toward and management of *time* sends often unintentional messages about you. When others are involved, you demonstrate respect for them by honoring time commitments. Punctuality is a quality especially appreciated in American culture. No amount of explanation or apology can make up for habitual disregard for time. Your adherence to time expectations in preaching is a special opportunity to demonstrate respect for others and creativity in making the most of the time available.

The Power of Nonverbal Communication

Verbal communication and nonverbal communication actually constitute two different languages. They operate according to different laws. In a face-to- face conversation, we are continuously receiving and sending signals of our thoughts, attitudes, and emotions. Most of these channels are nonverbal. As we have already noted, two-thirds of communication impact comes through nonverbal channels rather than the words we say. Let's summarize basic principles about the power of nonverbal communication.

In a face-to-face speaking situation, nonverbal messages dominate the communication. Studies in nonverbal communication have made clear that 65 to 90 percent of the impact of your communicating is determined by your nonverbal signals.[25] This research reminds us again that preaching is more than words. The time spent in preparation must not all be given to word crafting. The preacher must also give attention to preparing his own attitude about the message. If that message is not vital and meaningful to him, it probably will not be to his audience.

Nonverbal communication takes place whether a person intends to send a message or not. Some communication theorists hold that communication must be intentional to be genuine. Most, however, recognize that the majority of nonverbal signals others perceive in us are not only unintentional but even unconscious. This reality is another reminder to the preacher that his person is as important to his preaching as his presentation.

Nonverbal messages are received more rapidly and processed more quickly than verbal messages.[26] Many of the nonverbal channels are

---

Nonverbal Impact

In face-to-face speaking situations, nonverbal messages dominate communication.

Nonverbal communication takes place in spite of our intentions.

Nonverbal messages are received and processed more quickly than verbal.

While verbal messages are usually planned, nonverbal are more spontaneous.

While verbal communication is more intellectual, nonverbal is mostly emotional.

As the nonverbals of the speaker decrease, the nonverbals of the audience increase.

When words and nonverbal signals are in conflict, the nonverbal will be believed.

---

visual, like bodily movement, facial expressions, eye contact, and dress and grooming. These messages are received with the speed of light, even while words are slowly being formed. Other nonverbal channels are aural—tone of voice, pitch, rate of speech, melody, pronunciation. Though these are received more slowly than the visual, they are still more quickly perceived than your words. Your tone of voice tells the hearer something about you even before you complete a sentence.

While verbal messages are generally planned, most nonverbal messages are spontaneous. Of course not all verbal messages are planned. Sometimes we speak before we think and then regret it. We much prefer to measure out our words carefully and thoughtfully, based on what we hope to accomplish. Though that may be possible with verbal messages, the nonverbal messages do not wait for careful planning or conscious thought. They just happen, and usually the truth is out. It is for that reason that nonverbal signals are given such credibility.

While verbal communication is largely intellectual, nonverbal communication is mostly emotional. Our emotions seem to have a mind of their own. They surge up on their own in response to what is happening around us or to imagined conditions or events. Since the nonverbal channels mostly communicate emotion, they express it as it comes. The audience may grasp the preacher's ideas from his words, but they will understand his attitude and feelings about those ideas from his body language.

As the nonverbals of the speaker decrease, the nonverbals of the audience increase.[27] Myron Chartier tells of a D.Min. project in which a pastor preached a series of sermons in his normal style. Then, for a "control sermon" to test audience response, he read word for word from a manuscript, avoiding any bodily movement, eye contact, or vocal variety. The response of the congregation ranged from irritation to hostility. His supervisor for the project, a college professor, watched the audience carefully during the control sermon. He observed that they fidgeted, shuffled, read hymnals, looked around, and generally demonstrated boredom and distraction. He concluded that when the preacher reduces his nonverbals, the audience increases theirs. Stated positively, an animated delivery will capture attention and keep interest.

"Your tone of voice tells the hearer something about you even before you complete a sentence."

When your words and your nonverbal signals are in conflict, people will usually believe the nonverbal. The reason for this is that body language is much harder to fake than words. Insincerity or deception is signaled by such clues as a higher voice pitch, a slower than normal rate, more pronunciation errors than normal. Besides this, changed breathing patterns, sweating, and unusual eye movement can give you away as well.

In one experiment a speaker intentionally made his nonverbal signals contradict his words. Negative and hostile facial expressions and tone of voice were combined with pleasant and reassuring words. Then subjects in the study were asked what they thought was the real attitude of the speaker. The researchers reported that they depended only 7 percent on the actual words used. They depended about 38 percent on such features as tone of voice and rate of speech. The most credibility, 55 percent, was given to facial expression and other body language. Mark Knapp did not exaggerate when he wrote, *"How* something is said is frequently *what* is said." [28]

It is obvious that a preacher must give serious attention to the messages of nonverbal communication. Not only is he communicating nonverbally during his sermons, but he is sending nonverbal messages at other times as well. The elements of nonverbal communication will play a significant part in our study of preaching style in the next chapter.

Chapter Summary

Preaching is more than words. The nonverbal signals in preaching, often unintentional, have more impact on the audience than the content. The study of bodily movements is called *kinesics*, including posture and platform movement, gestures, eye contact, and facial expressions. Beginning with "home base" at the center, platform movements should then relate to sermon content. Gestures are best when natural and spontaneous. Facial expressions mainly communicate the preacher's attitude. Eye contact maintains a relational connection with the hearers.

Nonverbal communication related to voice and articulation is called *paralanguage*. More than any other factor, your voice determines the impression others have of you. External communication factors, such as clothes and grooming, are called *objectics*. The human use of space, *proxemics*, also affects communication. *Tactile communication*, person-to-person touch, is another key factor in nonverbal communication.

Nonverbal communication is a powerful element in the preacher's overall message. Nonverbal messages dominate the communication. They are often unintentional. They are received and processed quicker than verbal messages. They are spontaneous and mostly emotional. They increase in the audience as they decrease in the speaker. In a seeming conflict with your words, the nonverbals will be believed.

Review Questions

1. What is meant by *nonverbal* communication?
2. What impact do nonverbal signals have in speech communication?
3. What is *kinesics,* and what speech communication factors are included?
4. What guidelines does the author suggest for platform movement?
5. What do gestures contribute to speech?
6. Why are facial expressions considered highly credible by most audiences?
7. How does eye contact function in speech?

8. What is the impact of your voice in the way others "see" you?
9. Define *objectics* and *proxemics*.
10. What are seven principles that reveal the power of nonverbal communication?

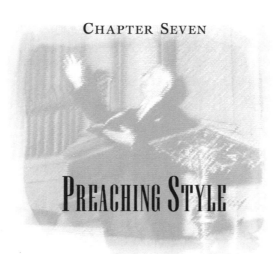

CHAPTER SEVEN

PREACHING STYLE

The preaching of our college pastor was dynamic. Not only the students but also townspeople crowded in to hear Brother Bill. He was animated, passionate, and strongly biblical. There was a dramatic flair in his sermons that captured our attention. When he came to a part of most importance, an idea that he felt strongly about, his voice would often break or tremble with emotion. I had not heard preaching with this energy and passion in all my nineteen years.

Sharon and I met at college, did some of our courting in that very church, and asked our pastor to marry us. After college we moved to Fort Worth to begin our seminary studies. One Sunday we drove the twenty miles to downtown Dallas to attend worship at the renowned First Baptist Church. There we heard a sermon by W. A. Criswell.

"Through the centuries the best known and most beloved preachers have had their sincere imitators."

I was amazed. The sermon was marvelous. It was animated, passionate, and strongly biblical, with a dramatic flair and a tremor of emotion in the voice. He preached just like Brother Bill. How could two pastors preach in such an identical way? We were perplexed for only a moment, then looked at one another knowingly as we remembered that Brother Bill had grown up in Dallas. He had apparently so admired Dr. Criswell that he copied his style of preaching.

This was not the first time an aspiring young preacher has listened to a great pulpiteer and said, "I want to preach like that!" Through the centuries the best known and most beloved preachers have had their sincere imitators. John A. Broadus broke new ground in his preaching style among Southern Baptists of the nineteenth century. His students at Southern Seminary ignored his warning not to copy another preacher. "Many of them tried to imitate his tones, his genuine pathos, his platform manner, failing to realize that they had only a few of his external characteristics and not the qualities of his success."[1]

Our purpose in this chapter will be to examine preaching style in its overall meaning and then look closely at its various features. The qualities that brought John A. Broadus success were qualities of character. His own devotion to God and love for people came through in his preaching. The style reflected the man.

Thinking about Style

In all the matters of sermon preparation and delivery, style seems to be the most abstract and elusive. We know different preachers preach in different ways. But how to define the differences and to evaluate the effectiveness of one style over another seems an invasion of personality and expression.

Personality is a key shaper of your style. Each of us is unique in temperament, physical features, habits of movement, outlook on life, social skills, self-perception, spiritual gifts, and the many other factors that make up the complex result we call personality.

Two erroneous views of style relate to personality. On the one hand is the view that preaching is a performance, that the preacher is really just acting a part. So he can look around and see who is best at it. Then

---

Def·i·ni'tion:
Style

A preacher's style is "his characteristic manner of expressing his thoughts, whether in writing or in speech."[2] The word is rooted in the Latin *stylus,* for pointed writing tool. Your handwriting is a unique expression of your individual style. By extension, your approach to oral expression—speech, language, physical movement, attitude—reflects your individual style.

---

he can try to copy the preaching style of someone he admires. We are all prone to copy others unconsciously, but modeling your preaching after someone else is not the answer to the challenge of style.

The opposite extreme is the view that the individual must be who he is and not tamper with any aspect of his unique approach to preaching. Since God made us, we are who we are by His hand. We must not attempt to be other than we are. So we really should make no effort at all to change our way of presenting a sermon.

As to the first view, let's make clear that preaching is not a performance. You are not just to play the part of the preacher for half an hour and then resume being yourself. Though it is most instructive to observe closely what effective preachers do to present their sermons, copying what you see in another preacher is not the answer for your style. Style includes who you are in your personality and in your walk with Christ. Preaching must be a genuine expression of your personality and your faith.

"You are not just to play the part of the preacher for half an hour and then resume being yourself."

On the other hand, however, we must not think that every aspect of your individual approach to preaching is an inviolable feature of divine creation. Your personality has been shaped by many forces—family background, home region, education, personal history, religious background, etc. Though we can affirm the providential hand of God in all these factors, we know that the basic thrust of the Christian life is growth and change into the new person God has created you to be.

The best approach to style, then, is to affirm that God does use a person to declare His message. This is the marvel of the principle of incarnation. God has decided to use people to do His work, and He knows we bring to that ministry all the baggage of our background. With the confidence that He can use even me, I will approach my preaching with a commitment to grow, to be the best I can be, to hope that the divine message which passes through my human personality will not be weakened, but affirmed and enhanced by the unique person I am.

STYLE AND SUBSTANCE

Contemporary advertising agencies are often called "image makers." Whether representing a major corporation, a political candidate, or an entertainer, their goal is to create a favorable image for their client in the mind of the public. They are not always concerned with whether that image is accurate. In fact, they often set out to create an image that is inaccurate in order to gain a more favorable response. Trial lawyers do the same thing to present their clients in the most positive light.

In this image making there is a separation of style and substance, of appearance and truth. Preaching, however, must not separate substance and style. The danger of this is clear in Jesus' warning to the scribes and Pharisees that they were "hypocrites," play actors. He likened their style to whitewashed tombs and their character to dead men's bones. For the Christian, the very nature of our faith and our message call for the wedding of style and content into one truth.

To examine this subject we might think of your manner of preaching as your style, your message as content, and your personal character as substance. This may be an artificial distinction of the usual meaning of content and substance as they are set over against style. My point, however, is that your manner of expressing yourself can be distinguished from your message and your character, and that message and character can be distinguished from each other.

> *"The very nature of our faith and our message call for the wedding of style and content into one truth."*

In spite of the fact that these three elements of preaching can be separated from one another in our thinking, they must be fully integrated in Christian preaching. The basic principle here is integrity. The sincerity and genuineness of the preacher are more effective in sermon delivery than any artificial features of style he could cultivate. No matter how we might try, we reveal our true character and attitude in subtle ways which can be read by our hearers. On the one hand I would encourage you to be yourself. On the other I would urge you to be a genuine Christian. When those two are the same, you have the foundation for effective style.

Affected Styles

Since we are talking about affected styles, that is, playing the part of the preacher, let me describe several artificial delivery modes I have heard as a teacher of preaching. In some cases preachers will follow one of these styles throughout the sermon. At other times they will slip into one of these patterns of speech at certain points in the sermon. Most of the time the preacher utilizes such a manner because he has heard preaching done that way.

Speech teachers have long spoken of the "ministerial tune." Stevenson and Diehl devote an entire chapter to this problem, describing it as an affected speech pattern that distorts several virtues of oral communication.[3] It is characterized by (1) a full volume projecting to the remotest hearer, (2) exaggerated articulation that is sound for the sake of sound, and (3) emotion that is overdone. Though difficult to describe, the ministerial tune is easily recognizable to most of us so that we say, "He sounds like a preacher."

There are several artificial preaching styles that some preachers adopt. Some are variations of that same "preacher" sound. The key to recognizing them is that the preacher does not sound like himself. He changes his speech when he preaches.

One artificial style is what I call the *ballfield yell*. Of all the patterns we mention here, this may be the most understandable. At the church picnic it's time to eat. The softball game must be brought to a conclusion. Someone waves with large gestures and shouts to the players in the field in a high, loud voice with a narrow range of pitch, "Come on in now; it's time to eat." That is the ballfield yell. Though it is appropriate on the ball field, it is not the best manner for preaching an entire sermon.

The second mode I would avoid can be called *the late night TV car commercial*. This is the hard sell. The car dealer is dressed in flashy clothes and delivers his urgent message loud and fast. He only has 30 seconds. Some preachers take on this "in your face" manner in their delivery because they want to put as much pressure as possible on the hearer. They *"We preachers would do well to talk like real people."* may gesture often with the pointed index finger, poking away at you until you expect to find fingertip bruises on your chest when you get home. This style is wearisome to the preacher and audience alike.

To be contrasted with the car commercial, however, is *the funeral director*. This style affects a "concerned" look on the face and moves slowly, as in a funeral procession. You are sure that this is serious business before the preacher says a word. And when he does speak, it is in a minor key. He may be loud at times and soft at others, but the entire message has the touch of gloom about it. When he speaks of "Gawd," the word rumbles as though it thundered. The Christianity preached may not be attractive, but it is dead serious.

A fourth style to avoid is *the devotional-intensive*. This is also a very serious style, and very religious as well. The manner reminds you of a counselor overplaying his part. In this mode the preacher affects a half voice, almost a whisper. He is like a caring friend who seems to be sincere and to have your best interests at heart but is taking your problems much more seriously than you do. Though this manner, sincerely applied, may be effective occasionally, it is quite annoying in large doses.

Several of these preaching modes may be included in what has been described as the "stained-glass voice." It is a manner only for church. It is a way of speaking only for preachers. The folk in the pew humor us because they reverence God and respect their pastor, but they might laugh out loud if someone talked like this in the real world beyond church. Our point is, of course, that we preachers would do well to talk like real people. The Bible was written in the language of the common man. We can preach it in the same way.

CONVERSATIONAL STYLE

The speech style I recommend for preaching can be called *conversational*. This does not mean chatty, light, or of little importance. It rather has to do with the communication emphasis of conversation. You might read to yourself, but a conversation requires another person. In a conversation the point is to express your ideas in such a way as to have the other person understand what you are saying. You are watching and listening and adjusting your comments to his response.

Conversational style is *dialogical*. It is a two-way flow of communication. Though the preacher may be doing the talking, the congregation is involved by their responses. Body language, facial expressions, "amens," and other comments provide feedback to the preacher who is in direct eye contact with his audience. He can tell when they are interested. He can sense when he is losing them. He can sense the "good vibes" of agreement or the "bad vibes" of hostility. They are in conversation though only one speaks.

Conversational style employs *the melody of normal speech*. All of us produce a certain tune as we speak. Our voices rise and fall in pitch so that a musician could chart the melody with music notes. Though the range may not be nearly as wide as singing, conversational speech has a tune which is pleasing and natural to personal communication.

> *"Variety is the spice of life and the sparkle of preaching."*

That is one of the problems with the artificial styles discussed above; the melody is unnatural and forced.

Conversational style is *personal*. The preacher does not talk *at* you but *with* you. He is not just unloading information, he is relating to you person to person. There is a level of warmth and intimacy which cannot be achieved in other styles of preaching. The sermon is designed to be hearer-oriented. The goal is not just to get it said but to have the audience understand, accept, visualize, and determine to act on the message. To accomplish this the preacher personally involves himself—his emotion, his conviction, his relationship with the audience.

Conversational preaching *allows for more variety*. Variety is the spice of life and the sparkle of preaching. Conversational style allows for variety in rate, pitch, volume, mood, and language. Just as in a stimulating conversation you may whisper and shout, rush and pause, laugh and ponder, philosophize and confess, conversational preaching expresses this same variety. There is room for drama and description, pathos and persuasion, argument and anguish. The aim of it all is to communicate.

In conversational preaching *movement is more natural*. Since the preacher is speaking extemporaneously, he is not tied to his manuscript. He can maintain good eye contact, one of the key features of good conversation. His facial expressions can be seen by the audience. He is free to use gestures which naturally emphasize his thoughts. He may step from behind the pulpit or use no pulpit at all. In all his movement his body language speaks alongside his words.

The conversational style is simply the preacher's natural manner. This means that the preacher uses his normal way of talking in the pulpit, enlarging his expression as necessary to reach his audience.

CHARACTERIZING PREACHING STYLE

Many factors contribute to the characteristic way a person expresses himself. Every preacher comes into the pulpit with all the baggage of his background, including qualities he has inherited from generations back. Education is a contributing factor to style, affecting vocabulary, demeanor, pronunciation, and other matters. Regional provinciality has its contribution to make in pronunciation, mannerism, slang, and your idea of how preaching is supposed to sound. Physical factors make for a particular voice quality, body movement, and facial expressions.

Style may tell a perceptive audience more about a preacher than the content of his preaching. Style flows out of the very character of the preacher. "A man's style cannot be separated from his modes of thought, from his whole mental character . . . for style, as Wordsworth forcibly says, is not the mere dress, it is the incarnation of thought."[4] Chartier emphasized the need for balance in style. Effective style can be cultivated, particularly if one is willing to risk self-disclosure and employ imagination.[5]

Though style seems to be a rather elusive and vague concept, the particular aspects of style can be examined for understanding it in more concrete terms. Haddon Robinson emphasized the need for a clear, personal, and vivid style.[6] Using the language of his own day, Broadus discussed three elements of style: perspicuity, energy, and elegance.[7] Writers who have followed since use simpler terms to say nearly the same thing: *clarity*, *force*, and *beauty*. In the following description, I will add other factors to these basic ones and construct a profile of preaching style.

Though styles should vary in differing situations and with different audiences, qualities of effective style will mark all good preaching. Some of these factors have more to do with the language of the preacher, some with his manner, some with his attitude. The audience perceives these factors by verbal and nonverbal signals in the preacher's delivery.

The chart identifies ten factors in such a way that you can evaluate your own style. Even though an evaluation of preaching is subjective at best, having others assess your style by the chart will help to identify weaknesses which can be strengthened.

A Profile of Preaching Style

	1	2	3	4	5	6	7	8	9	10	
Artificial											Natural
Stiff											Informal
Monotonous											Varied
Halting											Fluent
Timid											Confident
Harsh											Sympathetic
Flippant											Earnest
Obscure											Clear
Feeble											Energetic
Prosaic											Poetic

←——— less effective ——————— more effective ———→

The factors may overlap at some points, but each factor is distinct enough to be helpful in assessing the effectiveness of preaching style. To the right of the chart are the qualities that characterize good style. Opposite qualities are named at the left. The score runs from zero to ten. By grading each of the qualities, you can come to a style score.

Artificial versus Natural. A natural manner in preaching is more effective than any contrived style designed to "sound like preaching." An artificial manner is a way of speaking that no one would ever use in ordinary conversation or in any other normal communication situation. Without even realizing it, many beginning preachers "put on" certain patterns with their voices, gestures, posture, even facial expressions. The natural manner can be enlarged and intensified to accommodate public speech without loss of the natural element. I will have more to say about this later.

When I was a young person, I determined I did not want to be a preacher. One of the main reasons was that my pastor seemed to change his personality when he stepped to the pulpit. He became more "religious" sounding and lost the normally friendly and positive tone in his speech. It seemed to me to be an act. I couldn't understand how putting on an act like that was honest, so I decided I could never be a preacher.

> *"Today's audiences generally prefer a more informal style."*

Stiff versus Informal. The preacher is caught in a tension between being God's special messenger with a unique role and, at the same time, identifying with his audience as one of them. Today's audiences generally prefer a more informal style. An informal style is friendly, allowing the congregation to relax and identify with the preacher. Even in cap and gown at a graduation ceremony or in the serious atmosphere of a funeral, the audience responds better to some element of informality. In addition to signaling aloofness, a stiff formality can suggest indifference and weakness of conviction.

Different churches are used to different levels of formality in their pastor's manner. I preached as interim pastor for a year and a half in a church that was rather formal in its worship style. One of the women in the church called it "stuffy." I was told that the people would not respond aloud to the preaching. As I conducted the evening services in a rather informal manner, I discovered that they really enjoyed that relaxed approach. They began to get involved by answering questions, laughing at my humor, and making the sermon a two-way communication.

Monotonous versus Varied. Variety is the spice of life and of preaching. The most common complaint of audiences about public speaking is a monotone voice and dull presentation. Variety keeps the audience's attention and gives a dynamic to the ideas of the preacher. Variety is important in the rate of speech, tone of voice, pitch, volume, and mood. Variety is also best in gestures, facial expressions, platform movement, and other body language. A conversational style offers the best opportunity for variety.

C. H. Spurgeon warned in his lectures that preachers should never "indulge in monotones."

> Vary your voice continually. Vary your speed as well—
> dash as rapidly as a lightning flash, and anon, travel forward
> in quiet majesty. Shift your accent, move your emphasis,

avoid a sing-song. Vary the tone; use the bass sometimes, and let the thunders roll within; at other times speak as you ought to do generally—from the lips, and let your speech be conversational. Anything for a change.[8]

Halting versus Fluent. The idea of "fluency" calls to mind a river flowing along with consistency and power. Even though it may rush at times over the rocks and in the narrows, it is never hesitant and uncertain. Halting, on the other hand, is speech that reminds you of a boy who has just stumped his toe; he hops and falls, he mutters and groans, he stumbles and limps as he tries to walk. No doubt you have heard speakers who halted like that.

Fluency suggests expertise, competence, experience. A fluent speaker may pause, but it is for a reason. He may change his rate and volume, but the message continues. The halting speaker seems to pause because he cannot think what to say next. He stumbles and changes direction. He uses vocal pauses like "uh," and "umm." He uses unnecessary verbiage like "you know." All of this distracts from his message. Fluency comes with practice, good preparation, and absorption in your message.

Timid versus Confident. When the speaker is obviously not confident in his manner, the audience tends to be less confident of his ideas. Timidity in preaching suggests fearfulness and self-protectiveness. The preacher seems to be afraid of his hearers' response. This attitude contradicts the Christian message and undercuts the preacher's credibility. Confidence, however, suggests boldness and conviction. The preacher seems to be sure of himself and his message.

> *"When the speaker is obviously not confident in his manner, the audience tends to be less confident of his ideas."*

Credibility with the audience may well rest on the preacher's confidence in himself and his message. If he does not believe in his own calling and in the truth of his message, he will communicate that uncertainty in a number of ways. If, however, he seems to be confident in his preaching, the congregation is more likely to have confidence in him. They will assess his message to a large degree by his manner.

Harsh versus Sympathetic. Harshness as a manner of speaking suggests severity and insensitivity on the part of the speaker. In the voice, facial expressions, word choice, and other aspects of his manner, the preacher seems to be angry with his hearers. Harshness sets the speaker against his hearers and causes them to put up their defenses. He seems to be insensitive to them, to their needs, to their viewpoint. The preacher may not realize there is a hard edge to his voice and manner. He may just be intense about his message, with a sense of urgency and gravity that causes him to lash out at his audience.

Rapport with the audience is vital to effective communication. It is the friendship factor in the communication situation. Your hearers can sense, through all the signals they receive, what your attitude is toward them. Sympathy with their needs causes the audience to be open and receptive to the speaker. The sense that he understands and appreciates their struggles suggests that he may have an answer. John A. Broadus said more than a hundred years ago, "If I were asked what is the first thing in effective preaching, I should say sympathy; and what is the second thing, I should say sympathy; and what is the third thing, I should say sympathy."[9]

Flippant versus Earnest. Of all the qualities desired in the attitude of the preacher, none is more at the heart of preaching than earnestness. If the preacher does not seem to have a heartfelt commitment to what he is saying, his audience will not take him as seriously. A flippant and offhanded manner seems to suggest that the subject of the message is of no real importance. The nature of the Christian faith demands that those who preach it be personally in earnest about it.

Though today is the era of casual and laid-back communication styles, earnestness in preaching is still vital. One student preacher leaned on the pulpit and talked more like he was chatting about the nice fall weather than communicating biblical truths of eternal importance. He sounded a lot like Mister Rogers on the children's television program. Though he was talking about very serious concerns, his manner did not indicate it. It was really hard for the audience to take him seriously. You almost expected him to say, "It's a beautiful day in the neighborhood!"

Obscure versus Clear. The great fault of much preaching is fuzzy thinking. When the preacher is not quite sure what he is talking about, the audience can tell. Some may think ambiguous preaching is somehow superior. Broadus wrote, "A certain grand-looking obscurity is often pleasing to some hearers and readers, who suppose that it shows vast learning, or great originality, or immense profundity."[10] For most audiences, how-ever, the acid test of preaching is clarity. If the sermon is not clear, little else matters.

> "If the sermon is not clear, little else matters."

The first step toward clarity of style is precise thinking about the sermon subject. Sermon structure must also be clear, with carefully worded statements of your main points. Clarity is also aided by the use of common vocabulary. A professor in seminary used to tell us to use "people talk" in our preaching. By this he meant the normal words of the common man. Illustration is also important for clarity. Every sermon concept should be carefully illustrated in such a way as to picture the idea precisely.

Feeble versus Energetic. Energy in preaching style is expressed in animation, force, and passion.[11] Energy is first physical, indicating strength, health, and vigor. Energy in your preaching will result in movement—gestures, facial expressions, overall animation. Energy is also emotional, expressing enthusiasm, expectation, and passion. Beyond this energy is mental, with focused thinking and logical connections between ideas. Feebleness, on the other hand, is also physical, emotional, and mental. The congregation senses this energy or lack of it and responds accordingly.

The sense of authority in your preaching contributes to energy of style. Authority in preaching comes along two lines: the content of the message and the person of the preacher. Authority in content depends mainly on the biblical base of your sermon. Personal authority depends on confidence, knowledge, and passion. The greater the sense of authority in the preaching style, the more forceful it

> "Allow yourself the freedom to express your thoughts in grander ways."

will be in its impact. Argument also contributes to force of style. Remember that no one accepts ideas which are nonsense to him. Preaching is forceful when you offer the hearer sufficient reason to accept what you say.

Prosaic versus Poetic. The contrast of prose and poetry is common in literature. As a matter of style, preaching is more interesting and effective when it is poetic—with a flair about it, a touch of the dramatic, vividness of imagery, a sense of rhythm and climax. *Prosaic* means dull and commonplace, with the use of ordinary language without rhyme or meter. Too much preaching is like this—ordinary, with no drama, no use of the language in a dramatic and unusual way. This poetic quality in preaching is the beauty or elegance mentioned by generations of writers.

Beauty in preaching style has to do with the form and flow of the presentation, the realism and passion of the content, and the vividness and appeal of the imagery. There is much you can do to improve your preaching style in the area of beauty. Practice will help. Reading good literature will help. Allowing yourself the freedom to express your thoughts in grander ways will help. You can appeal to imagination with descriptions and pictures using concrete words. Appeal to all the senses—sight, smell, taste, touch, hearing. A concrete term is always more dynamic than an abstract one, the specific more dynamic than the general. Good structure lends beauty to your style. The mind of man moves naturally toward order and form and away from chaos and confusion. As symmetry is appreciated in poetry and architecture, so is it appealing in preaching. So plan your outline carefully and see that the flow of thought proceeds in an orderly fashion.

Your Many Styles

Though we have defined *style* as "your characteristic manner of expressing yourself," we must not conclude that your style as a preacher is set in stone. In one sense your preaching style is you. It is a reflection of your temperament, your personality. The features of your style are reflective of the unique set of characteristics that mark you as an individual person. Your style of expression allows people to distinguish you from others.

> *"For public speech enlarge and intensify your natural manner of speaking."*

There are sides of your personality, however, that you may not think are appropriate for the pulpit. Your sister overhears you dramatize a children's story to your nephews and laughs, "Well, that's a side of you

I never saw before." You get into telling funny stories at a men's retreat, and your laymen see a side of your personality you hadn't shown before. You talk it up in a basketball game with the college students, and they see a side of you they haven't seen in the pulpit. In each case you are communicating effectively in a style that is vigorous and colorful, but it is still *your* style.

Why not bring these colorful and communicative aspects of your personal style to the pulpit? Of course, there is a line you don't want to cross, a line of decorum and good taste, a line of sensitivity to audience expectations. But too many preachers have such a limited idea of preaching style that they never express themselves in the most effective way. Remember, the aim is to communicate and to do it in the best fashion. The message you preach is worthy of the full dimensions of your personality.

The greatest hindrance to improving preaching style is the discomfort you must experience to make any change. First, it is uncomfortable to admit that some natural mannerism is distracting. Anyone suggesting such a thing is criticizing your personality. But even if you admit the problem, you will have to behave in an uncomfortable way until a new habit is established. This means stepping outside your comfort zone. But it is necessary. In preaching as in athletics, there is often "no gain without pain."

Beyond efforts to improve style, for public speech you will also need to enlarge and intensify your natural manner of speaking. Obviously, your normal speech patterns must be adapted to the public speaking situation; you will speak louder, more slowly, with more exaggerated movements. These are the features of an *enlarged style*. The way you talk in a conversation across the kitchen table would be too quiet, too subdued, and too passive for public speech. Public speech takes more words, requires more time, needs larger gestures, more dramatic facial expressions, a louder voice, crisper articulation, and greater variety in rate, pitch, and mood. Several factors call for these adjustments.

Adapting Your Style

The *size of your audience* calls for modifying your style. Your aim is to reach the person farthest from you. Small-group communication calls for a different style than public communication. In a large crowd you do whatever you must to make the communication connection with the "guy on the back row." The size of the room is another aspect of this need to adapt. Brigance offered a mathematical formula to indicate how the distance to the audience and the size of the room in public speech dramatically affects what the hearer receives.[12]

An associate pastor made announcements so softly in the worship that I was sure he couldn't be heard. I told him to speak up, to address the farthest person. When he later asked me how he was doing, I replied that his comments probably reached to the seventh or eighth row now. If you will think of your projection in terms of distance, it might help to reach that farthest person. Do not let the false security of modern sound systems cause you to withdraw instead of projecting.

> *"But be sure you are adapting to the audience and not expecting them to adapt to you."*

Another factor for adapting style is *the nature of the audience.* You will not speak to a children's group in the same style you use at a funeral. Neither will you preach in your morning worship like you would at a youth rally. Your devotional at the nursing home will be short, loud, and to the point. Your address to the Lion's Club will not be in the same manner as a prayer meeting talk. In every case you will almost unconsciously adapt to your audience. But be sure you are adapting to the audience and not expecting them to adapt to you.

Other factors affecting your style are the *subject of your sermon,* the *occasion,* and the *location.* You will usually make these adjustments without having to plan them. If your are speaking in a natural manner, adapting to the situation will be almost automatic. This is one of the dangers of a contrived and artificial style designed to "sound like a preacher." That kind of style may leave you little room for adjustment. A conversational style, on the other hand, is your natural manner but can be adapted in any number of ways to suit the demands of a particular preaching situation.

If people are much aware of your style, it has intruded on the message and lost its rightful place. Style is the "packaging" of the message. Your preaching style should never be the remarkable element of your sermons. The priority is the message and its work in the lives of the audience. John Broadus wrote, "The best style attracts least attention to itself, and none but the critical observer is apt to appreciate its excellence, most men giving credit solely to the matter, and having no idea how much the manner has contributed to attract and impress them."[13]

"The best style draws attention away from itself to the content of the sermon."

Style is not a mere ornament to the sermon. The manner of the preacher carries such weight for the effectiveness of the sermon that your style can make or break it. You can package your message in the dull, listless tones of a stereotypical sermon mode. Or you can present the biblical message with the poetry, the drama, and the color it deserves. How you do it may well determine whether they hear you.

CHAPTER SUMMARY

Preaching style is the preacher's characteristic way of expressing himself. The best style is the most natural, without affectation or artificiality. Preachers can fall into a pattern called the "ministerial tune" or other unnatural ways of speaking that should be avoided.

Conversational style is dialogical, uses a normal melody, is personal, allows for more variety, and employs natural movement. Style has traditionally been characterized by such factors as clarity, force, and beauty. A chart in this chapter employs ten contrasting pairs of qualities to indicate less effective or more effective style. Better style for preaching is natural, informal, varied, fluent, confident, sympathetic, earnest, clear, energetic, and poetic.

Though the preacher will have a natural manner characteristic of him, he will use a variety of styles as he adapts to different audiences and preaching situations. Overall, the best style draws least attention to itself.

Now that we have considered the importance of preaching style, we will move on to a related subject, your method of presentation.

REVIEW QUESTIONS

1. Define *preaching style.*
2. What two errors about style relate to the preacher's personality?
3. What is a "ministerial tune"?
4. Identify four artificial styles that preachers should avoid.
5. What is meant by *conversational style*?

6. Identify ten sets of contrasting qualities that might be used to characterize preaching style.
7. What factors in the preaching situation call for adjustments in the preacher's style?

CHAPTER EIGHT

Effective Presentation

More than a hundred years ago, James Stalker expressed the sentiments of most students when it comes to sermon delivery.

> When I was at college, we used rather to despise delivery. We were so confident in the power of ideas that we thought nothing of the manner of setting them up. Only have good stuff, we thought, and it will preach itself . . . and many of us have since suffered for it. We know how many sermons are preached in the churches of the country every Sunday; but does anyone know how many are listened to?[1]

I hope, at this point in this study, you are convinced that sermon delivery requires your careful attention as a preacher. Even if you have "good stuff," as Dr. Stalker put it, the way you present your sermon may well determine whether it is heard.

After dealing with preaching style in the previous chapter, we still need to discuss the presentational method of the sermon. While style has to do with the characteristic manner of a particular speaker on a particular occasion, presentation method has to do with the way in which the content is presented in the sermon. There are five general forms of presentation that may be used for a speech: *impromptu,*

> "The way you present your sermon may well determine whether it is heard."

memorization, manuscript, extemporaneous with notes, and *extemporaneous without notes.*

The purpose of this chapter is to explore the question of your presentation method with a view to what is best for the preacher, the message and the audience. First, I will explain the five forms. Then I want to encourage you to adopt a method of presentation that will result in the best sermon delivery possible to you.

The Impromptu Sermon

An *impromptu* speech or sermon is delivered on the spur of the moment. It is spontaneous, without notes or preparation. Many business and professional leaders with extensive background and unusual expertise in their fields sometimes make no preparation for speeches. They know they can speak fluently and intelligently on their topic, whatever the time or audience requirements. Such speakers usually do not have the responsibility a pastor has for three or more new speeches a week.

Impromptu speaking has a number of problems that make it difficult.[2] The first problem is organization. The speaker must decide on the spot what he will talk about and what he will say about it. It is easy to wander in a muddle of comments about nothing much at all. A second problem with impromptu speaking is having to sift through all your information to sort, condense, and arrange it while you are talking. A third problem is that the audience can usually tell when the speaker is not prepared, suggesting that he didn't think the occasion worthy of preparation.

Sometimes, however, public figures, including pastors, are called upon to speak impromptu. It may be in response to a question that arises in a board meeting or church conference. It may be in the discussion period at the close of a Bible study. It may be at a gathering of the family after the death of a loved one.

When the need for an impromptu speech arises, keep these guidelines in mind. Make sure you understand the expectations of the audience or the question raised. Possibly ask for clarification to buy time. Quickly sort out the main ideas you want to cover. Be sure to keep it short. The audience will

"Keep a few outlines of sermons in the margins of key texts."

forgive your lack of fluency speaking off the cuff, but they will not appreciate your going beyond a reasonably brief time. If there are further questions, you can always say more.

You will have to make some preparations if you are determined to be ready "in season and out of season." One way is to keep a few outlines of sermons in the margins of key texts, with a quick recall list in the flyleaf. Though you may go years without having to use this backup system, it will be worth it that one time when you are called on out of the blue, as when the scheduled speaker does not show up at the men's banquet. Calvin Miller suggested being prepared like this, even being ready to switch sermons if the one you are preaching isn't working.[3]

The Memorized Sermon

In the study of ancient rhetoric, one of the basics of good speech-making was *memoria*, or memory. [4] Students in the Greek and Roman schools memorized long passages from literature and oratory so that they could recite them as needed in various speaking situations. In early American education students presented "declamations," memorized recitations of great speeches. Today memorizing longer passages of literature or oratory is not common. As a result, schoolchildren today are not required to learn the very words that carry great thoughts from history and literature.

Though there are some great benefits to memorization, especially of passages of Scripture, this is not an efficient and communicative method for speech communication. Recitation of memorized material does not have the spontaneity and vitality of unrehearsed speech. Even if a speaker memorizes his own words, they still sound memorized.

Very few preachers have ever sought to write out and memorize their sermons. The preparation time is great. The delivery style is usually unnatural. Adapting to the needs of the occasion and the audience is nearly impossible. The preacher of a memorized sermon becomes a performer instead of a participant in a two-way process. These disadvantages do not apply, however, to the use of brief poems, hymns, or other passages the preacher may want to memorize for use in his preaching.

133

The Manuscript Sermon

"Reading speeches is more common today than in any generation since Demosthenes faced the clamor of Athenian crowds."[5] Brigance suggested that this trend has arisen because of radio and television. The precise time constraints of the broadcast media seemed to require speakers to work from scripts to stay on schedule. Another reason for so much reading of speeches is for those in public life to avoid being misquoted. Reading is also prominent because business and political leaders are compelled to make speeches even though they are not trained in public address.

Some of the great preachers of past generations have read or preached from manuscripts. Thomas Chalmers not only read his sermon; he held it in one hand and followed it word for word with the index finger of the other hand. Nevertheless, one of his hearers said, "His eyes were afire with intelligence and rapture and zeal."[6] While not reading word for word, George Buttrick used a full manuscript which he consulted from time to time as needed. He was so effective in this method that he influenced a generation of students to do the same.[7]

Preachers who use manuscripts in the pulpit generally give two reasons for doing so: it gives them more security and enables them to be more precise in their language. Though these may sound like good arguments in favor of manuscript preaching, those who listen are probably not impressed. It takes a particularly gifted person to read without sounding like he's reading and maintain eye contact while looking at his manuscript. Most of us are not able to do it.

Manuscript preaching should be avoided for several reasons. For one thing, the preparation of a manuscript for reading is very time-consuming. Even though some preachers do prepare manuscripts without using them in the pulpit, they do not often write out every sermon if they have several to do each week. Public figures who must give a number of speeches each week usually have professional speech writers to prepare them.

A second reason manuscript preaching is to be avoided is the difficulty of maintaining a natural

> *"It takes a particularly gifted person to read without sounding like he's reading and maintain eye contact while looking at his manuscript."*

speaking style. The manuscript preacher is concentrating on "reading the words correctly" rather than on "expressing ideas meaningfully," as in normal conversation. Most important, using a manuscript is not conducive to spontaneous audience adaptation.[8]

I have heard some effective readers. They practice in advance. They turn their pages like a magician doing a trick. They even look at the audience a good bit. Even the best readers, however, still produce the "feeding chicken effect," their heads bobbing up and down from manuscript to audience. No matter how well they read, they are still locked into a method that leaves little room for interaction with the congregation.

EXTEMPORANEOUS PREACHING

It is obvious that there are serious drawbacks in the use of the *impromptu, memorizing,* and *manuscript* methods for presenting a sermon. The great majority of speech and preaching teachers would urge you to use the fourth method, *extemporaneous.* This word comes from two Latin parts, *ex* meaning "out of" and *tempus* meaning "time." English dictionaries often give the first meaning as "done or spoken with little preparation; off hand." This sounds like *impromptu.* But there is a significant difference.

In his classic book *The Art of Extempore Speaking*, M. Bautain, eloquent professor at the Sorbonne, wrote two statements about extemporaneous speech that reveal its character. "Extemporization consists of speaking on the first impulse; that is to say, without a preliminary arrangement of phrases. It is the instantaneous manifestation, the expression, of an actual thought, or the sudden explosion of a feeling or mental movement." Then he wrote on the next page, "We will devote our attention only to prepared extempore speaking, that is to say, to those addresses which have to be delivered in public before a specified auditory, on a particular day, on a given subject, and with the view of achieving a certain result."[9]

In modern speech communication the term *extempore* does not mean "off the cuff" as the word seems to suggest. An extemporaneous speech is one in which the speaker assembles his material, plans an outline, and may even rehearse his delivery. But he probably does not write a manuscript. He allows the specific language of the presentation to

---

Def·i·ni'tion:
Extemporaneous Preaching

A well-prepared sermon delivered with few notes or none at all is called "extemporaneous." The word literally means "out of the time" and emphasizes the spontaneity and freedom of the extemporaneous method. Though extensive study may be done, even a manuscript written, the speaker does not memorize the words of his sermon. He rather gets his subject and its treatment in view and trusts the word choice to the moment of delivery.

---

develop as he speaks. "That is the key: careful preparation and practice, but spontaneous language development."[10]

The difference between *extemporaneous* preaching *with notes* and *without notes* is so significant that I am identifying the two as different forms. Preaching with notes can be extemporaneous to a limited degree, but it also has much of the quality of manuscript preaching. The preacher is tied to his written material in either case. Depending on the extent of his notes, he may actually read parts of what he has written. His eye contact with the audience will be broken repeatedly, much more than he thinks. He will never quite get into the mode of a fully oral presentation, with all its advantages for effective communication.

Most of this chapter will be devoted to preaching without notes. In the course of the discussion, I will often lump *manuscript* preaching and preaching *extemporaneously with notes* together as I point out the advantages of using no notes at all. My basic premise is that preaching is an oral medium and as such is best when written material is not brought to the pulpit. Even the limited use of notes changes the nature of the presentation in significant ways and always has its impact on the audience. As we will see now, preachers through the ages have learned the secret of preaching without notes and profited from it.

THE WITNESS OF HISTORY

The advantages of extemporaneous preaching have been recognized for centuries. Augustine's preaching was usually without notes, recorded at the time by secretaries in the audience. His preaching was characterized in the ways often used to speak of extemporaneous preaching—spontaneous, simple, direct, and to the point, though he would digress from time to time.[11]

The Reformers of the sixteenth century often went against established methods and preached extemporaneously. John Calvin was a strong advocate of this method. "It is remarkable that one who was so scholarly in all his tastes should be the determined champion of extempore preaching. Indeed he went so far as to declare that the power of God could only pour itself forth in extempore speech."[12]

In Bern, Switzerland in 1667, church authorities instituted the Bern Preacher Act, which required of preachers that they give their sermons extemporaneously. It stipulated "that they must not read the same in front of the congregation from notes on paper, which is a mockery to have to watch and which takes away all fruit and grace from the preacher in the eyes of the listeners."[13]

George Whitefield, evangelist of the First Great Awakening, was one of the modern pioneers in preaching without notes. His preaching was dramatic and fervent, while his contemporaries often placed more emphasis on logic than passion for preaching. The professors at Harvard criticized Whitefield for preaching without notes, insisting that no strong argument could be handled convincingly without a manuscript. Whitefield responded that he loved to study as much as any preacher. "Preaching without notes," he said, "costs as much, if not more, close and solitary thought, as well as confidence in God, than with notes."[14]

Jonathan Edwards is famous for his sermon, "Sinners in the Hands of an Angry God," which he read from a very small manuscript held before his face. He was so nearsighted he had trouble reading his own writing so a young man held a lantern at his shoulder to give adequate light. Even though delivered in this manner, the sermon had a powerful impact. Later in life, however, Edwards advocated different methods, either memorizing or preaching extemporaneously.[15]

"The overwhelming weight of argument is on the side of extemporaneous preaching."

For many a preacher, the decision to preach without notes was brought about by an embarrassment in the use of a written manuscript. DeWitt

Talmage, on the first Sunday of his first pastorate in Belleville, New Jersey, laid his manuscript on a sofa on the platform. To his dismay, the manuscript slipped through an opening in the back of the sofa and fell inside. While the congregation sang a hymn, the preacher had to get down on his hands and knees to retrieve it. After one more embarrassment when the gas lights failed, he gave up the use of notes altogether.[16]

Many of the most able expositors have felt that notes would interfere with needed eye contact. Among them were G. Campbell Morgan and Alexander Maclaren. F. W. Robertson took very simple notes with him to the pulpit but rarely looked at them.[17] Even those who did not preach extemporaneously have recognized its advantages. R. W. Dale wrote, "It seems to me that the overwhelming weight of argument is on the side of extemporaneous preaching; but I have very rarely the courage to go into the pulpit without . . . notes."[18]

The first Southern Baptist homiletics professor, John A. Broadus, made it his practice to preach without notes. He would outline his sermons on lettersize paper, folded lengthwise. Then, after getting the ideas clearly in mind, he would leave the notes in his study. On one occasion, as he started toward the pulpit, he discovered that he still had his notes with him. He stopped and handed them to his daughter, and said, "Daughter, I forgot to leave my notes at home. Will you keep them until after the services?"[19]

Clarence Macartney, pastor of First Presbyterian Church of Pittsburgh for twenty-six years, was committed to preaching extemporaneously without notes. While a student at Princeton, he was invited to supply the pulpit of the Presbyterian Church at Prairie du Sac, Wisconsin. His first Sunday he tried to follow the advice of his homiletics professor, Dr. David J. Burrell: first, have a clear outline, and second, preach without notes. Though he took his manuscript with him that first Sunday, Macartney did not look at it. Nonetheless he felt it was a distraction and chained him to the pulpit. The next Sunday and every one that followed throughout his ministry he preached without any notes in the pulpit.[20]

Preaching without Notes

The prospect of preaching without notes can strike terror into the heart of a preacher. To be in the pulpit with nothing but a Bible and an idea is risky business. Surely we don't mean no notes at all? Not even a little slip of an outline!? Maybe the preacher can write a few words on the palm of his hand and still preach without notes? Isn't it possible that preaching without notes can so frighten the preacher that he cannot think and will make a complete fool of himself?

"To be in the pulpit with nothing but a Bible and an idea is risky business."

I have heard this kind of doomsday talk for years as I have urged students to preach without notes. The written material they take to the pulpit with them is a crutch, and they are sure they cannot walk without it. Their notes are like a pacifier to a baby. It offers no nourishment, but he is insecure and restless without it.

By preaching without notes, I mean no notes at all. The only thing you need is your Bible. In his book *Expository Preaching without Notes*, Charles Koller made a good case for doing away with pulpit notes. But he also offered a disclaimer when he wrote, "Preaching without notes does not mean that there should be no notes on the pulpit."[21] I realize that you may want to bring any quotations or statistics you need for your sermon. When you first begin to preach without notes, you may want a brief outline tucked away in the back of your Bible. But it is not wise to begin by using notes with the idea you will drop their use later. Much better is to get used to being without notes from the beginning.

Do not think that preaching without notes is a test of homiletical purity. Sermons are preached every week with manuscripts and outlines in the pulpit. I have heard many preached that way myself, and some of them were good. But they were not nearly as good as they could have been. Preaching without notes is best not only for traditional deductive preaching but for inductive forms as well. Ralph Lewis advocates extemporaneous delivery in his *Inductive Preaching*, especially preaching without notes, as best for connecting with the audience, a key aim of inductive sermon form.[22]

ADVANTAGES OF PREACHING WITHOUT NOTES

Preaching without notes has a number of significant advantages, both to the preacher and to the congregation. As you think of the special nature of oral communication, these advantages will be obvious.

1. Preaching without notes gives the preacher more freedom of expression. A sermon exists only in the preaching just as a song comes to life only in the singing. Since it is in that moment of truth that the sermon lives, it is then, rather than in the study, that the preacher must be at his best. Preaching without notes is as important for preaching as singing without notes is for opera or acting without notes for drama. Imagine how the audience would respond if an actor read his lines, his eyes glued to the script.

The necessity of a continuous reference to notes squelches the preacher's freedom to express his ideas. In normal conversation we express ourselves with animation, with enthusiasm, with drama and flair. That natural manner of communication is delightful for the speaker and interesting for the hearer. Imagine a conversation in which one party takes out a sheaf of notes and begins reading or refers to an outline for his next comment. What an awkward approach to conversation this would be. It almost eliminates the speaker's freedom to speak. It is the same with preaching.

2. Preaching without notes enhances audience rapport. In our reference to a normal conversation, you can immediately see what a set of notes would do to hinder effective communication. The relational element in communication is especially affected by the presence of notes. Today's audiences want to be addressed personally and informally. They like the feeling of having the preacher talk *with* them rather than *to* them or *at* them.

Rapport in preaching refers to the sense of harmony and connection the audience feels with the preacher. It is the friendship factor, the camaraderie, that sense of belonging in which the congregation accepts

"In unwritten sermons, spoken freely and freshly from the mind and heart, the preacher comes into an immediateness of relation with his auditors that never is attainable by him who is dependent on his manuscript. There exists a nameless something acting and reacting on the hearers and the speaker as they look into each others' eyes, that no skill in reading with stolen glances at the audience, can ever render possible."

E.G. Robinson, *Lectures on Preaching* (New York: Henry Holt, 1883), 194.

the preacher and feels accepted by him. Just as rapport would be hindered by the use of notes or a manuscript in conversation, it is also hindered in preaching. When a preacher is distracted by his notes, the audience feels that he is not as interested in them as in saying what he has planned. It is almost as though he has an affair with the notes and the congregation resents it.

3. Preaching without notes inspires careful preparation. Macartney writes of preaching without notes that "it takes more out of a man, both in preparation and in the preaching. Let no minister choose this method for any reason except that experience proves it to be the most effective."[23] Preaching without notes is not reserved for those with "the gift of gab." In fact, it is a most dangerous temptation for the preacher who is a ready talker to count on his gift with words.

Preaching without notes tests the preacher's grasp of his subject. When he knows he will be preaching in a fully extemporaneous fashion, he will prepare in a different way. He will avoid complicated outlines with sub-points and sub-subpoints. He will work for simple wording for his divisions. He will keep his explanations simple and his illustrations vivid. He will make sure he has a good grip on a clear idea and how it is treated in the text. Preaching without notes will enhance his preparation.

> "Once for all, let me say, that extemporaneous speaking . . . does not exclude the most thorough and perfect preparation. It may be abused by ignorant and indolent men; but it is not designed to diminish the necessity of extensive reading and careful thought."
>
> Matthew Simpson, *Lectures on Preaching* (New York: Phillips & Hunt, 1879), 173.

4. Preaching without notes enhances freedom of bodily movements. We have already noted that much of our communicating is through nonverbal channels. Only about a third of the communication the audience gets from the preacher comes through his words. When the preacher is tied to notes or a manuscript, he restricts the vital nonverbal signals. His gestures are limited, his facial expressions are weakened, his movement on the platform is hindered by his need for his notes.

Referring to the habit of some preachers of following the words of their manuscript with the index finger while they read, Henry Ward Beecher wrote, "A man who speaks right before his audience, without notes, will speak, little by little, with the gestures of the whole body, and not with the gestures of one finger only."[24]

Preaching without notes allows the preacher to have only his Bible in hand as he faces the congregation. He does not even need a pulpit or speaker's stand. He can be much more free and spontaneous in all his movements. This will help to capture and hold the attention of the audience. It will enhance his verbal message by the full use of nonverbal channels of communication.

5. *Preaching without notes enhances eye contact.* Eye contact is the most important element in nonverbal communication. When the preacher looks his hearers in the eyes, he makes contact with them in a way not possible otherwise. The eyes are the window of the soul. The audience can catch a better sense of the message through good eye contact, but they also catch a better sense of the preacher as a person.

A preaching professor was asked by a friend to evaluate his sermon one day as he attended worship. Later, when they discussed the sermon, the teacher asked the preacher how many times he thought he had looked at his notes during the sermon. He guessed maybe 20 to 25 times. He was shocked when told that his guest had counted 161 occasions when the preacher broke eye contact to look at his notes.

This report illustrates two truths about the average preacher. First, he does not realize how many times he looks at his notes. He is actually glancing at them some eight times as much as he thinks. They are a much greater crutch than he realizes. Secondly, however clever and unobtrusive he may try to be in looking at them on the sly, pulpit notes will draw his eyes away from the congregation. A manuscript or sermon outline in the pulpit is like a magnet to the eyes.

6. *Preaching without notes allows the preacher to respond immediately to the interests and needs of his audience.* Eye contact is not only desired by the audience for good communication, but it is important to the preacher as well. As he looks into the faces of his hearers, he is reading their response. When they are uncertain about what he is saying, they signal it with a frown or other facial expressions. When they are

very interested and in agreement with his message, their body language and facial expressions say so.

There is a circuit breaker in the mind of every hearer that trips when he is presented with too much abstraction. The preacher can see it in the faces of his audience when their interest flags. The eyes seem to glaze over, and the face takes on a lifeless look. Sometimes they begin to fiddle with purses, look through a hymnal, or make "to do" lists for later reference. When the preacher notices these signals, he can immediately respond with something to regain attention, something concrete and vivid, something personal and relevant.

7. *Preaching without notes gives full play to the preacher's personality.*[25] In the truth-through-personality model, oral communication always gives much more emphasis to the personality side than does written communication. God has chosen to use human agency to communicate his revelation. He intends the message to be wrapped in personality. The preacher's own life experience, his zeal, his earnestness about his message, his humor, his individual manner of expression— these personal factors can clothe the message in the human element and give it a face and a life for the hearers.

> "The most vital element in the persuasion of a congregation is the person who stands in the pulpit. In turn, the paramount qualification of the man in the pulpit is his Christian character."
>
> Batsell Barrett Baxter, *The Heart of the Yale Lectures* (New York: Macmillan, 1947), 288, 289.

When the preacher uses a manuscript or pulpit notes, he so affects his own style as to hinder the congregation from getting acquainted with him. If he preaches without notes, he will find himself much more expressive of his real personality. He will be more animated, more at ease, more dramatic, more likely to express himself in his normal manner. In this the congregation reads a sincerity, a warmth, a true sense of who the messenger is. As a result they are more receptive to his message.

8. Preaching without notes enhances joy in preaching. Time and again I have convinced student preachers to preach for their first time without notes. Even though they have begun with fear and trembling, they have found most often that after their initial nervousness they enjoyed preaching as never before. They report feeling as though chains were removed from their arms and legs, as though blinders were taken from their eyes.

Preaching without notes for the first time is an exhilarating experience. The fear of forgetting everything adds to the emotional alertness. Before long the preacher feels as though he can fly. He is no longer tethered to the pulpit. He no longer has to check the written outline to see what to say next. He is face to face with his congregation as never before. He is reading their response and adjusting to it. He senses the power of the moment of truth as the Holy Spirit shapes the sermon in the very preaching of it. Once a preacher experiences preaching like that, he can never go back to the bondage of pulpit notes.

9. Preaching without notes pleases the congregation. When audiences are surveyed, they always indicate that they hate boring speeches. Perhaps the distaste is even worse for sermons because they are of eternal significance. The Christians in the pew want their pastor to speak directly and personally to them. They do not want him to read to them. They do not want him to be tied to notes as though he doesn't know what to say. They want to see him animated and passionate. If they are to take his message seriously, they expect him to be in earnest about it.

The people the preacher addresses also want their pastor to be genuine. They want to see the same personality in the pulpit that they see in the fellowship hall. With good taste and proper decorum, they want their preacher to be himself. They want his caring concern for them to come through in the sermon. After all, preaching is a church matter. It

---

"A manuscript fetters and binds me, . . . and I long to push it aside and look away from it at the people; and every time I do look back at it again, I feel as though something has come between us, and broken the current between us."

David H. Greer, *The Preacher and His Place* (New York: Edward S. Gorham, 1904), 178.

is not a solo performance. They want to be involved in the sermon with the pastor. For all these interests on the part of the congregation, a manuscript or notes in the pulpit are a hindrance.

10. Preaching without notes allows the preacher to make much better use of the time available. The use of a full manuscript increased greatly with the advent of radio preaching. Program time was strictly controlled and the preacher had to stay on schedule. It was thought that preparing a word-for-word manuscript would allow the preacher to control his use of time. Today, however, contemporary radio and television personalities are much more likely to speak extemporaneously. Popular "talk" shows are a prime example. The speaker is able to control his time more easily when he does not have to follow a script.

Every preacher will, sooner or later, face the problem of having less time to preach than he expected. The music in a worship service will go too long. Some special presentation or announcement will take more time than expected. Though he usually gets to the pulpit at the half-hour, the preacher looks at his watch to find it is a quarter till. If he is tied to his notes or a manuscript, he may not be able to adapt instantly to the new situation. Preaching without notes, however, will enable him to edit his sermon as he goes and use the available time to the best advantage.

11. Preaching without notes enhances personal and spiritual power in preaching. When a sermon is completed in the study, it is like leftovers in the pulpit. That well-crafted manuscript or perfectly balanced outline cannot be a sermon. They are but the prediction of a sermon that may or may not take life. When the preacher takes his written materials into the pulpit, he tends to preach in written style. There is something electric and powerful about oral communication that cannot be matched in print. Paper is a very poor conductor of electricity.

Preaching is a supernatural means of communication. The Christian preacher was never intended to preach in his own power. He is to be in partnership with the Spirit of God. In the selection of the text, in its interpretation, in the organization of the sermon, in its development— at every phase the preacher can experience the illumination and inspiration of the Holy Sprit. Though vital throughout, this supernatural empowerment is most significant in the moment of truth when the sermon is presented.

When the preacher is preoccupied with a manuscript or notes, his aim is to be sure to say what he planned to say. He is bound to his written material. The sermon ideas are printed on paper rather than burned into his heart. They are static and confining rather than dynamic and living. When he is free of his written notes, he can allow the Spirit of God to edit his material as he preaches. He can communicate at his best, and prayerfully go beyond that to communicate in the power of the Spirit. Standing before his audience with Bible in hand to preach out of the overflow of Spirit and word is what preaching was meant to be.

RISKS OF PREACHING WITHOUT NOTES

I have given a good bit of space to the advantages of preaching without notes. Now will there be equal time? No. I am biased in favor of noteless preaching, so I cannot make as good a case for the negatives. To be somewhat fair, however, let's consider some of the risks of preaching without notes.

1. *Preaching without notes forces the preacher to choose his words as he preaches.* The chief advantage of a manuscript is that the preacher can select his words carefully and more precisely express what he wishes to say. Preaching without notes calls for planning the sermon design in such a way as to have the whole sweep of the presentation in mind, but the words used in the sermon are trusted to the moment of presentation. If a preacher prepares carefully, he may find himself often using the same terms he has in his notes or manuscript. But he does not try to memorize that wording.

With noteless preaching, the preacher might stumble over his words and not express himself as clearly as he did in the study. More thorough preparation can remedy this problem to a large extent, but probably not entirely. There will always be some preachers better than others at expressing themselves extemporaneously. This difference in ability is also apparent in the study. Since preaching is essentially an oral medium, the preacher is wise to develop his skills in oral communication. This may require that some of his preparation be oral as he practices aloud what he will say in the sermon. When balanced against the gain in eye contact and spontaneity, the possibility of being momentarily at a loss for words is worth the risk.

2. The preacher without notes might forget something he meant to say. This could also happen with notes, of course, as you lose your place in your manuscript or outline. But being there before your audience without any notes at all is a scary matter. The best way to face this risk is to accept it and be willing to make a fool of yourself. It is better to fail now and then without notes than to run the risk of being bound by them. If you draw a blank, you will probably be the only one who knows it, unless you look panic stricken. You will not likely forget anything vital.

You can deal with the possible loss of memory by planning the sermon without much memorizing to do. Keep it simple. Tie your thoughts directly to the text. Avoid quotations. Remember as well that the pause when you forget seems like hours to you but may be only seconds to the audience. Ed Young of Second Baptist Church, Houston, was asked what to do when you forget. "That's obvious," he replied, "You keep on preaching until you remember."[26] Clarence Macartney told of a country preacher who would forget where he was from time to time in his sermon. He had a ready remedy. He had memorized many verses from the Psalms he could quote until he remembered the next idea in his sermon.[27]

3. Preaching without notes risks the temptation to be lazy and substitute glibness of speech for adequate preparation. Someone might mistakenly think that if he has the "gift of gab" the preacher can preach without notes and does not need to prepare so extensively. As I have already said, the very opposite is true. Preaching without notes calls for more careful and detailed preparation. The preacher must literally saturate himself with his subject in order to be completely free from his notes. If he tries to preach with little or no preparation, his message will suffer, whether he uses notes or not. If anything, preaching without notes can motivate us to prepare more carefully and tie the sermon more directly to the Scripture text.

Unfortunately, many preachers rely heavily on that "gift of gab." Too often they think they are offering profound and spiritually significant comments as they babble along with bland platitudes and rehashed material from other occasions. The people deserve better than that. As I have just mentioned, all your preparation time must not be devoted to *what* you will say. Remember that the *way* you say it can have more impact on the audience than the content of your message. That impact is short-lived and fruitless, however, unless there is the lasting biblical message that only comes with preparation.

4. *The preacher without notes may overreact to signals of disapproval in the faces of his audience.* The greatly improved eye contact in preaching without notes means the preacher sees every frown, every shaking of the head, every expression of disdain or ridicule. He may be so disturbed by such negative reaction that he loses his composure. He may be tempted to try to appease his detractors by watering down his message. When he preaches from a manuscript, he may not know how his audience is responding and thus be insulated from their attitudes. Preaching without notes leaves him unprotected as he looks them in the eye.

Remember the word of the Lord to Jeremiah at his calling to preach. Here was a young man from a priestly family being called to address his nation with an unpopular message. "Do not be afraid of their faces," God told him, "for I am with you to deliver you" (Jer 1.8). The preacher should never enjoy a negative reaction to his sermons. At the same time he must be bold in preaching the Word of God without fear or compromise. If he preaches without notes, he can adapt to the feedback of his audience to clarify what he is saying and work his way around some of the barriers he detects.

As you commit yourself to expository preaching without notes, the way you prepare and design your sermon will need to meet the challenges of the extemporaneous method of presentation. You will prepare more thoroughly. You will design your sermon for an oral instead of written format. You will plan an audience-centered approach. Now that we have the matter of your presentation method before us, we will move on in the next chapter to a more detailed discussion of sermon design.

Chapter Summary

The preacher's method of presentation is the technique he uses to preach his sermon: *impromptu, memorization, manuscript reading, extemporaneous with notes* and *extemporaneous without notes.* The most effective method for preaching is *extemporaneous* speech, involving careful and thorough preparation, with spontaneous language in delivery. Preachers of the past offer a strong testimony for the extemporaneous method. Preaching is most effective without the encumbrance of manuscript or notes. Preaching is by nature an oral medium, and the use of any written material in the pulpit weakens the presentation.

Preaching without notes has several significant advantages: more freedom of expression, better rapport with the audience, motivation to careful preparation, more freedom of movement, better eye contact, more responsive to the audience, fuller expression of personality, more joy in preaching, preferred by the congregation, better management of time, and more personal and spiritual power.

The risks of preaching without notes may be turned to advantage: forced to choose wording while preaching, the danger of forgetting, the temptation to poor preparation, and the exposure to negative signals from the audience.

REVIEW QUESTIONS

1. Identify and define the five general forms of presentation which may be used for a sermon.
2. What should a preacher do when he is called on to speak without prior notice?
3. What are the reasons usually given for delivering a sermon from a manuscript?
4. What does the word *extemporaneous* mean as applied to preaching?
5. Why is extemporaneous preaching with notes distinguished from preaching without notes?
6. Identify eleven advantages for extemporaneous preaching without notes.
7. Explain the risks of preaching without notes.

CHAPTER NINE

DESIGNING THE SERMON

The idea of "designing" a sermon may never have occurred to you. Most of the time we talk about "preparing" sermons or "writing" sermons or "outlining" sermons.[1] One meaning of design is "to form in the mind, to contrive." As you think of preparing your sermon to preach extemporaneously, think of forming it to accomplish its purpose, of getting a mental picture of the idea of the sermon and the various aspects of that idea that are expressed in the text. This chapter will suggest several basic principles to guide you in planning your sermon design.

Structure for sermons may be characterized in several ways. The organization of the sermon can be basically *deductive* or *inductive*. This distinction has to do with the way the sermon moves between general truths and particular examples. Deductive moves from general to particular, and inductive does the opposite. Within these basic categories are many variables. The sermon can be organized as a *narrative* which follows the telling of the story. Another form of narrative structure is the *homiletical plot* suggested by Eugene Lowry.[2] The structure can also be based on a communication model such as Monroe's *motivated sequence* outline, which we will examine below.

"Create a presentation design that will allow the hearer to assemble the whole in his mind just as the preacher conceives it."

Whatever the structure of a sermon, the basic unit of design is a segment of thought. David Buttrick calls these modules of language "moves."[3] A segment is somewhat parallel to a paragraph in written material. It is one thought, a bundle of words offered to the listener to add one more piece to the unfolding treatment of the sermon idea. Imagine the preacher with all his ideas laid out on his desk as he prepares his sermon. He must put them in order, some subordinated to others, some generals and some particulars, all connected in some way to the one idea that controls the sermon. His aim is to create a presentation design that will allow the hearer to assemble the whole in his mind just as the preacher conceives it.

Any sermon structure should be characterized by at least four qualities.[4] A sermon with good structure will be *unified*, dealing with one subject that is limited enough to be manageable. Good structure involves *a discernible order*, following a sequence of ideas that not only presents the material in a logical fashion but appeals to the audience as well. Third, good structure for sermons utilizes *a balanced arrangement*, with main ideas of generally equal strength and development with balanced appeal. A well-structured sermon also *moves toward a specific target*. This means the sermon aims for a climax in thought and presentation. S. M. Lockridge suggested a climactic five-part plan characteristic of traditional Black preaching: start low, go slow, move higher, catch fire, quit in a storm.

Extemporaneous preaching without notes will call for a distinctive approach in your sermon preparation. In preaching from a manuscript you would concentrate on getting the wording right. If you preach with notes, you might write out the sermon, but you would also want to

> "The order and the parts of the discourse should be clearly fixed in the mind; illustrations may be selected and arranged; suitable language for certain portions may be well studied, or the whole sermon may be written; yet at the time of delivery, with a heart full of the subject, and with the outline clearly perceived, let the speaker rely on his general knowledge of the language and his habit of speaking for the precise words he may need."
>
> Matthew Simpson, *Lectures on Preaching* (New York: Phillips & Hunt, 1879), 173.

make sure your notes are legible and easy to follow. For extemporaneous preaching without notes, your focus in the preparation is not with the words or notes but with the overall concept of the sermon as it will be delivered.

Let me suggest several guidelines for preparing effective extemporaneous sermons. As you apply these suggestions, you will get the sermon clearly in view.

THOROUGH PREPARATION

Preparing sermons for extemporaneous delivery requires doing the detailed work of thorough preparation. You must be sure of your material. A common failure in preaching is having nothing of substance to say. If you are to preach effectively without notes, you will have to give yourself to preparation that is not only thorough but also of a different sort than for a sermon to be preached from notes or a manuscript.

For an extemporaneous sermon you are preparing the ideas and not concentrating on the words. Koller distinguishes between the visual memory and the logical memory in a preacher's grasp of his sermon.[5] If the preacher tries to remember what he has written rather than the logical development of his sermon idea, he may become confused in the details. Preparation for extemporaneous preaching best avoids extensive memorization. You are not trying to memorize words and phrases so much as to lay out the sequence of ideas in the sermon as they will unfold.

David O'Dowd of Reformed Theological Seminary compares a preacher's preparation to that of actors preparing for a play. The amateurs, he said, will memorize their lines, but the professionals will know the play. When a cue is missed, the amateur is at a loss because all he knows is his part. The professional can improvise because he knows the play. As extemporaneous preachers, we will not try to memorize the words, but we will know the sermon.

John Broadus advocated that preachers, especially in their early years, make detailed notes or even a full sketch of the sermon. He suggested going over these notes shortly before preaching to kindle the mind and heart and move the emotions by the subject to be preached. These preparation notes, however, should not be carried to the pulpit. Rather the preacher should get the whole of the sermon in his mind so that he "has stretching before him a well-defined track of thought, divided by natural landmarks into distinctive sections." His aim in preparation is "to get the track he is to follow so clear in his mental vision, that he can flash a single glance from beginning to end of it."[6]

Some of the greatest preachers seemed to spend little time in preparation. This might lead us to think little preparation is the best way, but two brief examples will show just the opposite. Charles Haddon Spurgeon prepared his Sunday morning sermon on Saturday night after seven o'clock. He prepared his evening sermon on Sunday afternoon. One of his biographers who knew him well said, in referring to this habit, that he did not so much prepare the sermon as prepare the preacher.[7]

> *"The material for my sermons is all the time following me and storming up around me."*

Henry Ward Beecher, one of the most outstanding preachers of the nineteenth century, began his preaching career with extensive word-for-word preparation of manuscripts. Finding little joy and freedom in delivering these sermons, he would occasionally abandon the carefully crafted manuscript and preach on a theme that had taken hold of him on Saturday. He said he did so to "get rid of it."[8] He finally came to prepare his sermons mostly on Sunday morning and Sunday afternoon. He always had a dozen or more topics developing in his mind during the week. He said, "The material for my sermons is all the time following me and storming up around me."[9]

Neither Spurgeon nor Beecher preached expository sermons. Spurgeon tended to preach out of his vast knowledge of Puritan theology, usually taking a one-verse text as the framework for his ideas. Beecher tended to draw on life experience for his inspiration. Their preparation was thorough and exhaustive, but it was not confined to a concentration on the immediate sermon at hand. They rather lived and breathed their preaching, constantly studying and observing. Then the task of assembling thoughts for a particular sermon was a quick and delightful one.

THE TEXT SHAPES THE SERMON

An expository sermon is based on a particular text. The text gives the sermon its theme, the primary theme of the text writer. The text also gives the sermon its treatment of that theme in the way the text writer treats it. This provides the sermon structure. In addition the text gives the sermon much of its supporting material from the text writer's development of his theme.

When the text shapes the sermon, the text can serve as the only notes needed by the preacher. Not only is it helpful to him to refer to the source of his sermon in the Scripture passage; it is also helpful to his audience. While they may resent his being preoccupied with a manuscript or notes, they will appreciate his repeated reference to the text as his sermon unfolds. Rather than a solo performance by the preacher as he presents his ideas, the congregation gathers around the Bible with him to hear a word from God.

When the text serves in this way as your sermon notes, you are not left without any written prompting at all. You can mark or highlight the particular words or phrases that carry your main theme and the key ideas about that theme in the text. In this way you have your outline, your subject, and your points. You will want to word these ideas so carefully and concisely that you have no trouble remembering how to state them. Keep them simple and direct so that a return to that phrase in the text will immediately call your statement to mind.

Do not use numbered subpoints. Keep your ideas simple and uncluttered. Not only does the congregation have difficulty keeping up with a complicated outline, but you will also not be able to remember it. This calls our attention again to the difference between written and oral communication. An outline may look very good on paper, with carefully alliterated points and subpoints, but be much too complex for the audience to follow. About the time you say "thirdly" for the second time, they are lost. They do not know whether you mean "thirdly" under "second" or "thirdly" as the third main idea.

"An outline may look very good on paper, but be much too complex for the audience to follow."

Take full advantage of all the developmental material in the text, whether used by the writer or only suggested. The Bible is full of figurative language. It has in almost every text words with vivid backgrounds and graphic meanings. The historical and cultural customs referred to in the text make for colorful development of your sermon ideas. The context of the chosen passage may offer additional developmental material. When you use the textual development to the fullest, you will have much less supporting material to create yourself.

Balanced Inductive and Deductive Movement

In recent decades, writers in homiletics have often addressed the problem of deductive movement in preaching. Ralph Lewis has advocated inductive preaching as an answer to the dull, academic, and tedious traditional sermon.[10] While making some very good points about the need for inductive preaching, Lewis painted a caricature of traditional preaching that is not accurate in my experience. Nevertheless, the debate is framed in terms of the difference between deductive and inductive sermons.

Two general characteristics distinguish between deductive and inductive preaching. In the first place, this difference involves the direction of movement in the presentation of the material. Deductive thinking begins with general truths and moves to specific examples of those truths. Inductive thinking begins with specific experiences or examples and moves to general conclusions. So, if a sermon generally begins with the biblical truth as a starting place and then moves to specific applications and illustrations of that truth, it would be deductive. If it begins with specific examples and life experiences and moves from there to general truths, it would be inductive.

Beyond the direction of movement in a sermon, the kind of material employed will indicate whether it is inductive or deductive. All sermon material could be classified as *generals* or *particulars*.[11] This is the difference between a general statement of truth like "love your neighbor" and a particular example of such a truth in action like the story of the good Samaritan. Deductive preaching tends to be overburdened with generals and weak on particulars. Inductive preaching is heavy on particulars and light on generals.

All preaching can have a combination of deductive and inductive movement. On the one hand you can make a point and then support it (deductive). Or you can give an example and then tell the truth it illustrates (inductive). As far as movement is concerned, the preacher does well to begin with his audience where they are. The opening of the sermon will always be best in the inductive mode, with particulars. But the preacher will also want to move deductively, with a clear statement of his sermon divisions followed by supporting details.

As far as the kind of material we use, Lewis made an excellent point in calling for more concrete and specific development. Any sermon, whatever its direction of thought, will be dull and uninteresting if it does not use a good bit of down-to-earth life experience particulars. Lewis says inductive preaching like that of Jesus involves a lot of personal references, human need, parables, stories, narrative logic, common experiences, visual appeal, questions, dialog, and so forth.[12] There is no doubt that good preaching will utilize these "inductive" elements. But good preaching will also involve clearly stated biblical truths.

> "The preacher does well to begin with his audience where they are."

Oral Communication Style

Written and oral communication generally follow different patterns. Not only is this true in matters of style, but it is also true in the design of the presentation. In written communication you can use various fonts, bold print, underlining, and other means to place emphasis on ideas. In oral communication you can use your tonal and body language to place emphasis. In written communication the reader may go back to reread something he did not understand, while in oral communication the hearer has only one chance to hear each sentence.

In written communication you are limited by space, while in oral communication you are limited by time. A sermon unfolds in time, one segment of thought following another. The hearer must assemble these thoughts in his own mind for the whole message. As a result, the order of your presentation is very important. You must plan carefully what you will say first, and next, and next. This may be one of the most important aspects of your preparation. Koller wrote that "the preacher commits to memory a progression of thought rather than words, and is never tied to a particular phraseology."[13]

> "A sermon unfolds in time, one segment of thought following another."

This progression of thought may be seen in a normal sermon outline, but there is more to it than just an outline. You will use transition statements between divisions. You also know what will take place within each division. You will use development designed to function as *explanation, illustration, argument,* and *application.* Though this order of development has logical and communication appeal, your presentation can mix the four kinds of development in various ways. Usually you will begin a division with *explanation* and finish it with *application.*

The special nature of oral communication design requires you to plan your sermon carefully as an unfolding sequence of ideas in time.[14] Like a walk in the countryside, your sermon must take your hearer step-by-step along the journey of thought in a way that gets his attention and keeps his interest. Think of the sermon as made up of segments of thought one to two minutes in length. Your use of the four elements of development will determine many of your segments. Each of these segments has a completeness about it, but each is linked to the one before it and the one after it like cars on a freight train.

SIMPLICITY AND CLARITY

The great fault of much preaching is fuzzy thinking. If the preacher is not quite sure about what he is saying, we must not expect the audience to come away with a clear idea. A preacher may think he is clear in his own mind about his ideas but not be clear in his efforts to communicate those ideas in the sermon. An idea clearly grasped is an idea clearly expressed. It is only through clear expression that the preacher is sure of what he is thinking.

Most of us are not naturally gifted for analytical thinking. We usually think in the comfortable zone of general notions and never worry too much about splitting hairs over ideas. Gifted or not, however, a preacher should try to develop the skills of clear and precise thinking. The theological ideas in Scripture are often stated in highly technical and precise terms. The Greek language of the New Testament allows that kind of precision. So does English. But the preacher will have to make those fine distinctions in his own study before he can make them in his sermons.

Clarity is one of the most important elements for effective extemporaneous preaching. Without clarity, the preacher's passion, fluency, depth of thought, and energy are nearly irrelevant. An unclear message can rarely accomplish its purpose. The whole point of preaching is communication. The preacher wants to relay the message to his audience so that they understand it, accept it, visualize it, and determine to act upon it. If it is unclear, none of this is likely to happen.

> "The great fault of much preaching is fuzzy thinking."

The first step toward clarity in preaching is precision in your own identification of the sermon theme. For biblical preaching, which allows the text to shape the sermon, it is vital that your understanding of the subject of the text be clear. The beginning place for that understanding is a careful analysis of the words of the text. The writer had something in mind when he wrote those words. Our task is to discover what he had in mind and name that subject carefully, then make it the subject of the sermon.

Sermon structure must also be clear if the sermon is to be marked by clarity. The line of progression in a traditional rhetorical outline should be spelled out in clearly stated sermon divisions. The audience is helped at every transition to know where the preacher is going and what has been said thus far. In a narrative sermon, the story plot must unfold clearly and logically. This is "hearer-friendly preaching," which seeks to cover the whole distance to the hearer and not force him to work so hard at listening.

Clarity and simplicity are also aided by the use of common vocabulary. A seminary professor urged his students to use "people talk." By this he meant the normal words of the common man. Theological terminology can always be "translated" into more easily understood words for the sake of the children who might be present (and most of their parents).

Sermons are clearest when the preacher uses vivid language. This is simply language which draws pictures in the minds of the audience. Vivid language is concrete, specific, and descriptive. It appeals to the imagination. Every sermon concept should be carefully illustrated in such a way as to picture the idea precisely. Illustrations that are close but not quite exact for the idea always leave the hearer with a bit of confusion. A picture is worth a thousand words, but it doesn't take nearly that many words to draw a picture in the imagination of the audience.

A Balanced Audience Appeal

Effective extemporaneous preaching will appeal to the various members of the audience and to the various dimensions of the human psyche. The appeal to imagination mentioned above is only one of the appeals a sermon should make. It should also appeal to reason, to volition, to understanding, and to emotion. Some in your audience will respond better to one appeal, others to another appeal. Men respond to certain appeals, women to others. Various age groups like different approaches to putting your ideas across.

Central to your appeal is sermon development, your supporting material. *Development* means the preaching you hang on your outline. As mentioned above, there are basically four kinds of development: *explanation*, *illustration*, *argumentation*, and *application*.[15] As you study your text, you will be

> *"High predictability will result in low impact."*

watching for material that functions in one or more of these ways. The writer is communicating in the same way you will in your sermon. He is appealing to the whole man—the intellect, the imagination, the reason, and the volition. Make sure your development is balanced with these elements, filling in with other material to augment what the text writer gives you.

A balanced appeal also calls for supporting material of various kinds. Your illustrations can come from your personal life, but not too much. They should also come from contemporary events, historical references, from nature, family life, sports, agriculture, homemaking, medicine, politics—every area you can use. Especially note the particular interests of your congregation, the kind of community they live in, the kind of jobs they have. Frame the ideas of your sermon in terms of their experiences as much as possible.

An important factor for a balanced appeal is the careful use of language. The words you use can be *predictable* on the one hand or have *impact* on the other. Hesselgrave described the problem of predictability in preaching, "The sermon that is simply a series of generalizations capped off with a familiar illustration will not only be soon forgotten, it will probably not be 'heard' in the first place."[16] This is the kind of preaching we have all heard, in which you can almost complete every sentence for the preacher. It is the "same old same old." That kind of sermon cannot have impact on the audience. High predictability will result in low impact.

The key to impact is to frame the old story in new terms. Use some imagination. Try to see and hear and touch and smell the biblical stories and the contemporary illustrations. Avoid overuse of generalities in favor of a good portion of particulars. Keep everything you say down-to-earth with examples, applications, and specific details. Work for freshness, the kind of novelty and originality that make your sermon ideas sound new and interesting. High impact requires low predictability.

In balancing your appeal, also be careful about calling for a response to the gospel based on self-centered and carnal interests. An appeal to trust Christ as Savior may often seem to be based on self-interests. The benefits promised for accepting the salvation of God are attractive indeed. But the real aim of the Christian life is to glorify God. You can touch a nerve and get a hearing by dealing with your hearer's needs, but always call Christians to the higher calling of the lordship of Christ and the glory of God.

A Motivating Sequence of Thought

Most of the time we think of structuring a sermon in such a way as to follow a logical presentation of the sermon material. In this pattern an introduction is for laying the groundwork for your ideas, giving background, defining terms, perhaps offering a historical sketch. After such an introduction you offer your sermon thesis and proceed to prove that thesis from a text or texts. At the end of the message, you may offer appropriate application. But this pattern is not attuned to the audience.

The oldest sermon form is the *homily*, a verse-by-verse walk through the sermon text with explanation and some application along the way. The homily does not require a thesis. In fact it may not even identify a subject. The assumption is that the text subject will be clear enough as you go through it. This can be an effective way to deal with a text, but it still follows a logic-driven presentation sequence.

If a sermon is to be biblical in rhetorical mode as well as content, it will begin with the contemporary audience. Every prophet in the Old Testament sought to address his own contemporaries in terms of their situation. New Testament writers did the same. The Epistles of the New Testament are largely written to address specific needs in particular churches. They all express a consciousness of the situation of the readers and their relationship with the writer.

"Begin the sermon with the present day, not with the ancient world of the Scripture."

If we preach in this way, we will want to design our sermons in terms of the interests and needs of the audience. We will want to begin the sermon with the present day, not with the ancient world of the Scripture. The Word of God is eternal. Its theological truths are timeless. Why should we not begin with the present day and its circumstances? We will use application for the audience at some point in the sermon. Why not begin with their life experiences, take them to the text for answers, and show them how these timeless truths can be applied today?

Allen Monroe has suggested a design for persuasive speech he called the "motivated sequence."[17] This pattern is designed according to the way the audience thinks. There are five phases to your sermon in this design, each one containing a whole group of thought segments. You begin with getting your hearers' *attention* to the subject. After the segments in this brief cluster unfold, you move to the *need* phase, in which you connect your subject to the needs of the audience. The third phase is *satisfaction*, designed to address the problems raised in the need step. The satisfaction phase is the bulk of your sermon, with more segments than all the rest together. Fourth is *visualization*, in which you imaginatively picture your hearer living out the sermon truths. Fifth is the *action* step, when you give the hearer specific steps he can take to implement the sermon idea.

If you will plan your sermon with the motivated sequence in mind, you will know at any point where you are in the flow of ideas. The main body of your sermon is the *satisfaction* step. In that section you are following the text treatment of its theme as your outline. The *attention* and *need steps* are your introduction, the *satisfaction* step is your sermon body and the *visualization* and *action* steps make your conclusion.

KEYS TO PREACHING WITHOUT NOTES

So far in this study of sermon delivery, I have given a lot of space to extemporaneous preaching without notes. It is my conviction that there is no other method as effective for the preacher. I also believe that any preacher can learn to preach his sermons without notes and maximize the powerful effect of the oral communication medium.

As we close this chapter on sermon design, let me go back over some ideas we have already considered and suggest four keys that will greatly help in preaching without notes: (1) thorough written preparation; (2) thorough oral preparation; (3) the text shaping the sermon; and (4) an oral presentation design. I can assure you that if you will follow this plan you can preach without notes and experience all the benefits of that method.

Key #1: Make thorough written preparation. You want to study your text so carefully that you understand its background, context, language, theology, and rhetoric. Then you will plan your sermon just as carefully, based on the message of the text, the nature and needs of the audience, and the dynamics of oral communication. You want your sermon material to be fresh, challenging, and clearly biblical. All of this is the *content* side of your preparation and will always require a lot of writing.

> *"Your first aim is not to find a sermon, but to understand the original meaning of the text."*

Working on paper is an important key to getting the text writer's ideas clearly in view and clarifying your own ideas. There is no substitute; you must write, write, write. Do not think you will sort out your sermon material by merely thinking about it. Only as you try to put your thoughts into words will they become clear. Some of what you write will end up in the trash. Don't let that bother you. Just get your exposition of the text on paper and continue to sort it out until it takes shape for a clear presentation.

Key #2: Make thorough oral preparation. When we think of sermon preparation, we usually mean the writing of the sermon material. But remember that a sermon is an oral presentation. Since you do not expect to read your sermon, shouldn't you give some preparation time to the oral delivery? After you have your content well prepared, take a walk and talk it out from memory. Maybe you prefer just pacing about your study. Recall the important aspects of the content and speak it aloud.

You may think of this *talking it out* as practicing your sermon. You will discover, however, that the sermon will change and grow as you speak it. Certain terms will come to mind, certain phrases, new illustrations, better ways of saying what you want to say. In this sense, you are not practicing a completed sermon, you are still working on completing it. Your written preparation should never be the only experience you have with your sermon ideas before you preach. When you go to the pulpit you should have already expressed your ideas orally as part of your preparation.

Key #3: Let the text shape the sermon. This means you make sure your sermon idea is the same theologically as the text idea. The text will reveal its idea and its treatment of that idea. As a result, your sermon idea and your divisions are all right there in the text. Much of your supporting material is also stated or implied in the text.

When you go to the pulpit with your Bible, the biblical text becomes your written outline. You may want to highlight or underline the phrases that are the basis for your sermon divisions. You will work carefully to word the theological ideas you want to communicate in the sermon. Though they are based on phrases or clauses in the text, they will have to be worded as complete sentences for the contemporary audience. This wording should be as simple and direct as possible so that you will not have trouble remembering it. It should so obviously reflect the text that a mere glance at the phrase you have marked will bring that wording to mind.

Key # 4: Plan an oral presentation design. Think of this design as a template, a pattern to follow that will allow the sermon to unfold in the most effective way. This pattern will provide a dependable order of presentation that will keep the audience with you while dealing effectively with the text material. It will include opening and closing material, transitions, division statements, and balanced supporting material—all set out in a time line of unfolding segments. It will not contain complicated material like subpoints that look good on paper but confuse the hearer.

If you follow a narrative design, you will want to keep in mind the way a story usually unfolds—*situation, stress, search, solution,* and

164

(new) situation. You can also explore other design patterns. The aim here is that you have the pattern clearly in mind so that as you preach your sermon, the sequence of ideas will unfold in an orderly manner. Since you have already saturated your mind with the text material and prepared a good contemporary expression of its ideas, your design model will guide you in an orderly way as you preach.

If you will follow these four suggestions, you can prepare to preach without notes—thorough written and oral preparation, text shaping the sermon, a clear oral design. Now we will consider the goal of all the preparation, the preaching moment.

Chapter Summary

Designing the sermon means to shape it according to its purpose, placing the idea and the whole presentation in order. Good structure is unified, orderly, balanced, and purposeful. Extemporaneous preaching requires a distinctive design. This can be accomplished with thorough preparation, allowing the text to shape the sermon, balancing inductive and deductive movement, using an oral communication style, working for clarity and simplicity, planning a balanced audience appeal, and using a motivating sequence of thought.

From the qualities of good design, the keys to preaching without notes are thorough written and oral preparation, allowing the text to shape the sermon, and planning a clear oral design for the order of presentation.

Review Questions

1. Explain the meaning of *sermon design.*
2. What qualities should mark effective sermon structure?
3. What is the focus of preparation for effective extemporaneous preaching?
4. What does it mean to allow the text to "shape the sermon"?
5. What is involved in the call for more "inductive" preaching?
6. How do oral and written style usually differ?
7. How can the preacher work for clarity in his sermons?
8. What are the steps of the "motivated sequence" outline?
9. What keys does the author suggest for preaching without notes?

CHAPTER TEN

THE PREACHING MOMENT

I t all comes down to this moment, the *moment of truth*. It is now that you must stand before the assembled crowd and declare the Word of God.

> Here is the final test! Here you win or lose! All that has gone before helps or hinders, as the case may be, but the proof of the pudding is in the eating. Here in the delivery of your sermon the nourishment which you have brought for a hungry congregation is either eaten with relish, satisfaction, and resultant strength, or it is left on the plate as a bit of cold victuals, useless and repellent. Take heed how you deliver![1]

These words from Charles Reynolds Brown ring true as we face the moment of truth, the delivery of the sermon. Everything finally is decided here. It is only in the preaching that an idea, an outline, a manuscript, becomes a sermon.

When we understand what preaching is in God's purpose, we do not rush to the pulpit rashly. We do not think ourselves preachers simply because we say we are. Rather "the burden of the Lord" is upon us. We preach because it is God who has called us to it. Listen to the warning of Karl Barth to the young preacher.

> What are you doing, young man, with the word of God upon *your* lips. Upon what grounds do you assume the role of mediator between heaven and earth? Who has authorized

you to take your place there and to generate religious feeling? And to crown it all, to do so with results, with success? Did you ever hear of such overweening presumption, . . . such brazenness! . . . Who dares, who can, preach, knowing what preaching is?[2]

So we are back to that question of Paul, "Who is sufficient for these things?" (2 Cor 2.16). When we think of preaching, we know none of us is qualified to handle the Word of God. Yet we must. It is our calling. Paul also said, "Woe is me if I do not preach the gospel" (1 Cor 9.16).

"It is only in the preaching that an idea, an outline, a manuscript, becomes a sermon."

We come to this *moment of truth* in faith. We know that we are able to preach because He is able. Though we will do all we can to develop our skills and prepare carefully, we still approach the preaching moment with a mixture of eagerness and uneasiness. Before we close this study, think with me about some of the issues to keep in mind as you come to the preaching moment.

CLARIFYING YOUR MOTIVATION

Why do we preach? For one answer to that question we can examine the preacher's inner drives. Jeremiah said, after declaring he would preach no more, that he was compelled to preach, that he had fire in his bones (Jer 20.9). Jahaziel burst out in prophecy to shatter the quiet of a solemn prayer meeting because the Spirit of God came upon him (2 Chr 20.15). Isaiah saw God in the Temple and was touched with fire from the altar (Isa 6). These and many other examples show that preachers are often forced to preach by an inner compulsion.

Is it enough to say, "I have to preach"? You have heard the admonition of experienced preachers, "Don't preach if you can be happy doing anything else." Is your own happiness the test? If so, many who have spent a lifetime preaching have missed the point. The ministry is not always a happy experience. There may be times when you would rather do anything but preach. But you must anyway. We must make sure that inner desire is the call of God and not the drive of ego. Can this inner compulsion be our reason for preaching?

A second motivation in preaching on any given day might be to get the word out. You may love to study the Bible, to find word meanings and historical background. You may really think it important that the Word of God be understood. Like Beecher, you may feel the need to preach to get rid of the ideas that swirl about in your mind. But the question must be raised again. Is getting the word out the primary aim of preaching?

A third focus for motivation in preaching might be to meet the needs of the hearers. If they are disheartened, you hope to encourage them. If they are confused, you hope to give guidance. If they are lonely, you want to assure them of God's presence. If they are in sin, you want to call them to repentance. Homiletics books have long discussed preaching aims in terms of the hearer's response. When you think of the needs represented in any congregation, it is most reasonable to think of your purpose in terms of the audience.

"We must make sure that inner desire is the call of God and not the drive of ego."

Why preach? Is it to satisfy an inner compulsion of the preacher? Is it to communicate the content of biblical truth? Is it to meet the needs of the hearer? Or perhaps we could name a more obvious fourth focus of motivation: to obey God as His servant and messenger. The answer is not so simple, but it is clear that each of these centers of purpose is valid. It seems to me that the immediate functional purpose of preaching is to communicate. Beyond that there is a larger overarching purpose.

The overarching aim of preaching is to call the hearer to faith in God. Whatever the subject, a call for faith is appropriate. Whatever the needs of the audience, trusting God with them is the best possible remedy. Preachers, however, seem to prefer *do-better* preaching over *trust-God* preaching. Most sermons focus attention on man and what he must do instead of God and what He can do. But Scripture and experience demonstrate that calling for faith is basic to all other purposes for preaching.

The hearer of your sermon can only make progress in the Christian life as he lays hold of God in faith. In turn, he can only lay hold of God on the basis of what he knows of God. "Faith comes by hearing, and hearing by the Word of God" (Rom 10.17). The basic response to the Word of God is to believe it and act upon it. Preach for faith!

How You Feel

"Should a preacher feel strongly about every sermon?" This question was raised by a pastor in a preaching workshop. My response was, "If you don't feel strongly about a sermon idea, don't preach it. Preach something you feel is important and has some urgency about it." At the time I thought that was a pretty good answer. The trouble with that answer is that it may have different meanings for different preachers.

For one preacher, enthusiasm reflects his own delight in discovering something "new" in the text. Especially for the preacher with a primary gift of teaching, the word studies and historical research excite him and make him eager to share the gems of biblical wisdom he has discovered.

Another preacher feels strongly about his sermon because it comes out of his own devotional life. He has met God in these ideas and wants others to meet Him there as well. He may use terminology like, "God has given me a message to share with you today." I recently heard a sermon like this on intercessory prayer. It came out of the preacher's life and carried a lot of passion as a result.

Feeling strongly about a sermon may mean something different still for a third preacher. His enthusiasm comes from his confidence that the sermon directly addresses the needs of the congregation. A pastor who lives among his people week after week cannot help but notice their struggles. As he prepares his sermons, he imagines that they gather around his desk, there to plead with him to give them spiritual food. When he plans a sermon for such needs, its ideas touch him at a deep level.

> *"The text is a constant that keeps preaching from being nothing more than a report on the preacher's own pilgrimage."*

Another kind of strong feeling about a sermon may relate to the preacher's personal experiences of conflict and frustration. He is eager to preach because he has prepared a sermon designed to confront the problems and weaknesses of the church. He wants to straighten out his critics, rebuke his church leaders, or light a fire under the "dead wood" segment of his congregation. His passion may be righteous indignation, resentment, or anger.

So what is the answer? Should a preacher feel strongly about every sermon he preaches? I wish it could be so. Passion in preaching is such a necessary element. I also wish that his passion could arise out of an intimate personal relationship with Christ rather than out of his own frustrations.

We have seen that effective preaching requires a balance of truth and personality. There is no separating the preacher's own experience from his interpretation and presentation of a text. Nevertheless, the text is a constant that keeps preaching from being nothing more than a report on the preacher's own pilgrimage. "For we do not preach ourselves, but Christ Jesus the Lord" (2 Cor 4.5). If we preach Christ, our passion about the message will depend on our personal walk with Him.

The Communication Mix

As you come to the preaching moment, remember that you are communicating over a number of channels—before, during, and after the sermon. You cannot *not* communicate. Every movement, word, vocal tone, facial expression, and gesture is sending messages. Your clothing, grooming, mannerisms, use of space and time, and social graces are all communicating something about you. All of the these channels of communication affect the way your audience perceives you. How they perceive you, in turn, will affect the way they receive your message.

Even away from the church you are communicating who you are and what you think. A well-known pastor, whose sermons were heard on television every Sunday, was in a restaurant with his wife. He was telling her something of a serious nature that had him concerned. As he talked, she reached out to put her hand on his arm. "Bob," she interrupted quietly and sweetly, "you're not smiling." He responded somewhat sharply that he wasn't intending to smile. "But someone in here probably recognizes you. Someone is probably watching. You don't look like you're trusting God very well now, and you can't explain it all to whoever might be watching." That pastor leaned back and relaxed a

"Anyone who claims to have the answers should be ready for some questions, even if they are never vocalized."

bit. He smiled at his wife. "You are right," he said. Then they continued their conversation.

You may think it isn't fair for you to have to live your life in terms of other people. But remember, it isn't your life. Also remember that you are communicating anytime someone can see or hear you. You will not always be able to explain what you mean by all those signals. We are brought back to the point I have made repeatedly: you cannot be one kind of person and another kind of preacher.

In a sense you live in a glass house. Your life is open to every watching eye. That is part of what it means to be in a public role like the ministry. It is even more critical for you because you are presuming to tell your neighbors week after week how they should live their lives. Anyone who claims to have the answers should be ready for some questions, even if they are never vocalized.

This may trouble you, as it does me, because I don't want to be acting a part for the approval of the crowd. I want to be honest, to be open, to be vulnerable about my own struggles and my failures. If I have to pretend I am happy when I am not, isn't that hypocrisy? Do I have to smile in restaurants because someone might see me? These questions are serious ones. Maybe an answer lies in Jesus' words, "Let your light so shine before men, that they may see your good works and glorify your Father in heaven" (Matt 5.16).

Wherever you go, your light is shining. Whatever you do, you are on duty. As long as you are representing Christ, you want to reflect positively on Him. There will inevitably be some misunderstanding about what you say, but try to keep your words clear. There may also be misunderstanding about what you communicate without words, but try to keep that clear as well. You are communicating, even unconsciously, who you really are. The unintended messages you send may well determine how your intentional messages are received.

Persuasion and Change

A sermon is a persuasive speech. You hope to persuade your hearers to change their beliefs, their attitude, and their behavior. You are justified in this desire to influence others because you are persuading them in terms of the very Word of God. Just as important as the truth you present, however, is your own attitude and manner in presenting it. We might call this your *stance*. Whether your hearers allow themselves to be persuaded will largely depend on this *stance*.

Let me describe two kinds of *stance* that may be taken by preachers as they attempt to persuade their hearers. One is the *adversarial* stance. It can be defined by understanding the New Testament word *adversary, antidikos*. The word comes originally from courtroom usage and means "opponent" or "enemy." An adversarial stance in preaching is one in which you accuse and charge, setting yourself against your hearers as their opponent before the law.

In a different position altogether is the *exhortative* stance. This stance is clear from the verb *parakaleo*, most commonly meaning "beseech," "comfort," and "exhort." The word comes from *para*, "with" and *kaleo*, "to call." The noun form is used of the Holy Spirit when He is referred to as the "Comforter." This stance brings you alongside your hearer rather than against him, exhorting him rather than accusing him.

An *adversarial* stance may actually create in the hearer a defensive response in which he resists any change. Your accusations may cause him to strengthen his commitment to views he may not have held firmly before. He will find "reasons" he didn't need before and actually dig in more as a result of your attack. If your stance puts you on one side, with him and his behavior on the other, he may identify with the error, just as you have identified him with it. Another common response to an adversarial stance is to find fault with the preacher personally.

If you really wish to separate your hearer from his wrong thinking, you must take a stand that will have him identify with you and your ideas, instead of clinging to his error. Place yourself on the side of your

---

Persuasion and Stance

Vital to the effectiveness of persuasive speech is the *stance* of the speaker. *Stance* is basically the attitude of the speaker concerning his message, his audience, and his own relationship with them. The audience will respond to a speaker according to his stance.

Preachers commonly take one of two stances: (1) exhortative stance, characterized by encouragement, and (2) adversarial stance, characterized by accusation.

hearer, with the wrong thinking and behavior on the other side. In this stance you are for him, so he will not feel attacked and see no need for erecting defenses.

Jesus took both of these stances in His ministry. With the ordinary people, the "sinners and tax collectors," He took an *exhortative* stance. He was obviously *for* them instead of *against* them. When He was criticized for eating with these undesirables, Jesus said He came not for the righteous but to call sinners to repentance (Luke 5.32). Toward the scribes and Pharisees, however, He took an *adversarial* stance, accusing them of being "hypocrites" (Matt 23). He said they were guilty of breaking the law of God while they pretended to be more righteous than others.

With those whose hearts were hard, Jesus was the prosecuting attorney. His stance was *adversarial*. With those He expected to change, He was the *exhorter* calling them to repentance. In His *exhortative* stance Jesus appealed as a friend. In His *adversarial* stance, He pronounced judgment on those who refused to change.

> "*Always stand with the people against the sin that ensnares them, not against the people and their sin.*"

There may come a time when your audience has refused the Word of God and will not change. If so, you may assume an *adversarial* stance. Be very careful, however, before you give up on God's people. When you must preach judgment, always do so with a broken heart. Hold out for repentance. Pray for change. Trust the Spirit to convince your audience of sin, righteousness, and judgment. As a pastor or evangelist, always stand *with* the people against the sin that ensnares them, not *against* the people and their sin. Stand with the Holy Spirit as an *exhorter*.

Adapting during the Sermon

Knowing your audience is essential to effective preaching. As you come to the preaching moment, you will know any audience in the general sense that you know human nature. If you are a guest speaker, you will do an audience analysis while you wait to preach. As you look out across the group, you will make quick assessments about age breakdown, gender balance, socioeconomic status. If you are a pastor, you will know your flock even before the moment of sermon delivery comes.

Whatever the level or thoroughness of your audience analysis, you will adapt your preaching to them. Like Paul, let your philosophy be, "I have become all things to all men, that I might by all means save some" (1 Cor 9.22). Whether you know them well or not, you must always be ready to adapt to your audience during the sermon. Your immediate aim is communication of the biblical truth. Your larger aim is to call for faith in the hearer. Neither purpose can be attained without reading your audience and adjusting to them.

You will adjust to the size of the audience and the acoustical qualities of the place. For public speaking your natural style must be *enlarged* to fit the audience. Your volume, rate, articulation, gestures, facial expressions, and other factors are all intensified to reach the most remote hearer. You will also adjust to distractions in the room—a baby crying, poor sound equipment, loud fans.

Your best presentation method for audience adaptation is extemporaneous preaching without notes. As you look your hearers in the eyes throughout the sermon, you can adjust quickly to their responses. If you are distracted yourself with manuscript or notes, you may well miss the signals that alert you to needed adaptation.

The nonverbal (and sometimes verbal) signals of your hearers will tell you about their response to what you are saying. If they look bored and distracted, they probably are. Some may seem perplexed. Others may look as though they do not agree with what you are saying. Still others may seem to think your comments unworkable and foolish. You may see that cynical, "I've heard it all before" look.

Remember, there is a circuit breaker in the human brain that shuts down attention when there is too much general and abstract material in a sermon. Keep your sermon well balanced between statements of truth and all the concrete supporting material that explains, illustrates, argues, and applies those truths. If you offer one general or abstract statement after another, you will see the attention lag. This is a signal to you to get down-to-earth—tell a story, give an example, make an application, get in touch with real life.

Managing Your Time

Another important way you adapt to your audience is the careful management of your time. Audience expectations as to sermon length will vary from place to place. You will want to find out what the local custom is and preach accordingly. In doing so, you show respect for the people and win their appreciation and attention. Remember, there are no bad short sermons. The content of your message will be received much better if you do not make it longer than the time allotted.

I was to be the closing speaker at an evangelism conference in Portland. My subject was heaven, and I had a good sermon ready from Revelation 4. The preacher before me preached on hell and took much more than his allowed time. As his sermon went on and on, the conference leader became more and more tense. He had made a point to write each of us about staying on time. At the close of the "hell" sermon, the preacher gave a long invitation to see if he could get the pastors and other church leaders present to be saved. There was no response.

By the time he was finished, it was 8:45 P.M. The meeting was supposed to be over at 9:00. A solo was sung and my time to preach came, with only 11 minutes to go. We had been there long enough that day and I was determined that we would be out on time. So I preached my four-point sermon on heaven in ten minutes. To do so I had to use only the best material and to move quickly through the sequence of ideas. It was wonderful. Everyone thought it was one of the best sermons they had ever heard. I was something of a hero.

"Always quit when your hearers wish you would continue, rather than continuing when they wish you would quit."

On another occasion at a similar meeting in California, I was second from the last preacher of the evening. As I got up to preach, I somehow lost track of the time. I was under the impression that I had extra time for some reason. As a result I preached much too long and the person after me had to cut his sermon short so he could catch a plane. The conference leader was fit to be tied. But this time I was the villain. It was a lesson I won't soon forget. I am responsible for the time I take as a steward of the grace of God.

I have heard preachers criticize the congregation for not being willing to stay longer to hear the Word of God. This seems to me a rather arrogant attitude to take. No one should insist that everyone sit there and listen to him as long as he wants to preach. Most sermons that go too long are not well prepared. It is easier to preach too long than to cut it short as needed. It is not the audience that needs to make some changes; it is the preacher.

Just as being late for an appointment suggests that you have little respect for another's time, so preaching too long indicates a lack of respect for the time of a whole audience. Some of those in a morning service may have appointments that require getting out on time. The parents of restless children in an evening service may have to get them up early to catch a school bus the next morning. It is up to you to be sensitive to these possibilities. If God turns a service into real revival, no one will mind staying. If you turn it into a marathon, they will.

Your Pulpit Perspective

One of the hazards of the preaching ministry is the faulty pulpit perspective many preachers develop. By pulpit perspective I mean your attitude and intention as you step to the pulpit. The incarnational model for preaching places as much emphasis on *personality* as on *truth*. Though your pulpit perspective can be corrupted by your misunderstanding of the truth, it is the human factor that most often causes the trouble. Consider some of the aspects of our humanity that adversely affect our pulpit perspective.

Preaching is a divine-human endeavor. Nothing you do so reflects your walk with God as your preaching. Nothing you do has you more concerned that God involve Himself in the effort. You hope that He will use you, preach through you, empower you, not allow your humanity to befoul the message. And when a sermon falls flat, it is not easy to dismiss your feeling of failure. You promise to prepare better next time and to pray more. You go home discouraged, maybe even depressed. You were the key to the whole worship hour, and you failed.

> *"Preaching discloses the Word of God, but it also discloses the preacher."*

Preaching also involves personal risk. Nothing opens your life, your heart, your thoughts, your faith to others like your preaching.

Preaching discloses the Word of God, but it also discloses the preacher. Nothing exposes you to the judgment of others like your sermons. Even when you do not hear their comments, you know that your congregation is constantly sizing you up on the basis of your preaching.

Since we are all naturally subjective anyway, it is easy to see how preachers can become so self-absorbed in their preaching. They are thinking about their own performance, their fear of failure, their desire to be effective, even impressive. I have heard prayers before a worship meeting that reveal this perspective, "Lord, just use Your servant. Let me declare Your word with power. Don't let the people see this preacher, but only You. Hide me behind the cross." And so the prayer goes, heavy with first-person references.

There is an inherent self-centeredness in each of us. We can dress it in pious poses and phrases, but it is still carnality. The filling of the Spirit is marked by an expansiveness, an others-centeredness, a God-centeredness. It is never marked by self-centeredness. So self-centeredness in your pulpit perspective is not an indication of the Spirit's filling. When you are occupied with your feelings, your concerns, your thoughts, your experiences, you may think there is something spiritual about it because you feel so strongly about it. But remember, self-centeredness is not of the Spirit.

In the preaching situation the hearer is the important factor. Without the hearer there would be no need for the Bible, the sermon, or the preacher. God's intention for preaching is to make Himself known, not for the preacher's fulfillment, or to utilize the Bible, or to empower sermons. God makes Himself known because He loves the people and wants to call them to Himself in faith.

As you approach the pulpit, keep this perspective. Pray for the people. Ask God to minister His word to His people, to meet their needs. You will not know all the hurts, the hopes, and the heartaches of those gathered before that pulpit. You do know you cannot meet all those needs. This is God's business. Most of the time you will not even know what He is doing as He takes His word to the hearts of those you face.

Think about the people, the "whosoever" of God. Pray for the people. Weep over the people. Study the people. Focus on the people and their needs. The sermon is for them. The hour is for them. "Lord, what do your people need to hear from You today? What do You want to

> "Freedom from self; that is the preacher's first, and last, and deepest need. Given that, he is free indeed. The dark shadow that hovers over his best work is his own shadow. He never finds himself until he has lost himself."
>
> William Pierson Merrill, *The Freedom of the Preacher* (New York: Macmillan, 1922), 132–133.

make known to them? How do You want to meet their needs? Show me Lord. Involve me in what You want to do. Do not let me be so absorbed in my thoughts and notes and text that I miss what You are doing. Feed Your people, Lord, from Your Word."

Anointed Preaching

The one thing I desire more than anything else as I step to the pulpit is the anointing of God. I like the story of the preacher at an evangelism conference many years ago in Dallas. The conference was closing with an altar call. All across the front of the auditorium were men on their knees. Various ones prayed aloud with urgency and passion. The words that stayed in the minds of many were prayed by a preacher from West Texas in a western cut suit and boots. He raised his arms and cried out, "Lord, help me to feel when I git home like I feel now."

"We must not confuse the anointing of God with emotion."

There have been times when I wanted to pray a similar prayer as a service closed. I was caught up in a movement of the Spirit of God. Everything had come together and the sermon had seemed to have a real anointing on it. "Lord, help me to feel next time I preach like I feel now." There is nothing like being God's messenger when God really speaks. There is nothing like having passion in your sermon that catches like fire to everyone in the room. There is nothing like offering an invitation when people really respond.

I have preached on other occasions when God really moved among the people but my own emotions were strangely flat. It was as though I was a step removed from the situation, impassively watching God at work but thinking it nothing unusual. I was grateful to see His word bear fruit. It was just that the emotion was not there for me. We must not confuse the anointing of God with emotion.

The Spirit of God wants to honor the Word of God every time it is preached. I am not sure He is so eager to honor a few devotional thoughts from the preacher's mind. Neither does He seem to want to empower the wrath of a preacher against his people or the antics of one trying to work up a contrived fervor. When the Word of God is preached humbly and prayerfully, I am convinced the Spirit will do His work.

It is obvious that the extent to which God works to empower preaching depends to some degree on the audience. Even Jesus could do no mighty works in His hometown for their unbelief (Mark 6.5). He pronounced woes on other towns as well, saying that pagan cities would have repented in sackcloth and ashes if the same witness had been given in them (Matt 11.21). I must not, however, lay the blame for powerless preaching on the congregation. Though I am unable to control the spiritual interest of the audience, I can make sure that I seek the Lord for His power on the preacher.

The anointing of God for preaching is God's business. But you can seek it. Determine to be a godly person—walking in intimate fellowship with Christ, trusting Him completely in all things, obeying Him without question or hesitation. Do your sermon preparation in communion with God. Expect Him to open the text and reveal the hearts of the congregation to you.

As you walk to the pulpit, forget all but the people to whom God wants to speak through you. Ask not that you speak well but that they hear His voice. Ask not that you remember your points but that the Spirit edit the sermon. Ask not that you have the power of God on you but that the living and powerful Word of God do its work. In that you will experience the *moment of truth*.

> *"Though I am unable to control the spiritual interest of the audience, I can make sure that I seek the Lord for His power on the preacher."*

Chapter Summary

It is only in *the moment of truth*, in the act of preaching, that the idea, the outline, the manuscript become a sermon. Though the preacher may be variously motivated, the overarching aim of biblical preaching is to call for faith. A preacher's passion about his sermon can be a hindrance unless it comes from right motives. Unintended nonverbal signals in or out of the pulpit send a message that affects how the sermon is received.

A preacher's stance toward the audience will dramatically affect their receptivity. Even during the sermon, adaptation to the audience is important. A key area of adaptation is the careful management of the time available for the sermon. The preacher's perspective in the pulpit is best focused on the audience and their needs rather than on himself and his performance. Anointed preaching is used mightily of God as the word and the walk of the preacher are in harmony.

Review Questions

1. What are some common motivations for preaching?
2. What danger lies in the desire for feeling strongly about every sermon?
3. How does a preacher communicate even when he is not preaching?
4. Distinguish between *adversarial* and *exhortative* stances and how they affect persuasion.
5. How can the preacher adapt to his audience during the sermon?
6. Why is time management during the sermon so important?
7. How would you describe anointed preaching?

ENDNOTES

CHAPTER 1

1. Fred B. Craddock, *Preaching* (Nashville: Abingdon, 1985), 52.
2. R. Albert Mohler, "A Theology of Preaching," *Handbook of Contemporary Preaching* (Nashville: Broadman, 1992), 14.
3. Craddock, 52.
4. Clyde E. Fant, *Preaching for Today* (New York: Harper & Row, 1975), 26.
5. David J. Hesselgrave, *Communicating Christ Cross-Culturally*, Second Edition (Grand Rapids: Zondervan, 1991). See Hesselgrave for a thorough discussion of seven factors to consider in cross-cultural communication.
6. H. J. C. Pieterse, *Communicative Preaching* (Pretoria: University of South Africa, 1987), 6.

CHAPTER 2

1. Phillips Brooks, *Lectures on Preaching* (New York: E. P. Dutton, 1898), 8.
2. Warren W. Wiersbe, *Living with the Giants* (Grand Rapids: Baker, 1993), 83.
3. John R. W. Stott, *The Preacher's Portrait* (Grand Rapids: Wm. B. Eerdmans, 1961).
4. Fant, 29.
5. Matthew Simpson, *Lectures on Preaching* (New York: Phillips & Hunt, 1879), 166–67.
6. Aristotle, *Rhetoric,* trans. Rhys Roberts (Chicago: William Benton, 1952), I:2:4, 13.

CHAPTER 3

1. William D. Brooks and Robert W. Heath, *Speech Communication*, Seventh Edition (Dubuque, Iowa: Wm. C. Brown, 1993), 239.

2. H. L. Hollingsworth, *The Psychology of the Audience* (New York: American Book, 1977), 21.

3. Michael Sack, "The Multiplex Congregation," *Leadership* XVI:4 (Fall 1995): 31.

4. Alan H. Monroe, et. al., *Principles and Types of Speech Communication*, Tenth Edition (New York: HarperCollins, 1996), 98.

5. Judy Cornelia Pearson and Paul Edward Nelson, *Understanding and Sharing*, Sixth Edition (Dubuque, Iowa: Wm. C. Brown, 1994), 250–54.

6. Steven A. Beebe and Susan J. Beebe, *Public Speaking: An Audience-centered Approach* (Inglewood Cliffs, N. J.: Prentice Hall, 1991), 67.

7. Alice Matthews, "He Said, She Heard," *Leadership Journal*, XVII:4 (Fall 1995), 50.

8. Monroe, 84–85.

9. Brooks, *Speech Communication*, 269.

10. C. H. Spurgeon, *Lectures to My Students* (Grand Rapids: Zondervan, 1955), 128.

11. Ibid., 128.

12. Ibid., 130.

Chapter 4

1. James H. Henning, *Improving Oral Communication* (New York: McGraw-Hill, 1966), 7.

2. See the following speech communication texts for a good explanation of various models: Ronald B. Adler and George Rodman, *Understanding Human Communication*, Fifth Edition (Orlando, Fl: Harcourt Brace, 1994), 14-18; Gail E. Myers and Michele Tolela Myers, *The Dynamics of Human Communication*, Sixth Edition (New York: McGraw-Hill, 1992), 10-15.

3. Claude Shannon and Claude Weaver based their "mathematical theory of communication" on Norbert Weiner's concept of "cybernetics." See Hesselgrave, 40.

4. Eugene Nida, quoted by Hesselgrave, 91.

5. Pearson and Nelson, 10, 11.

Chapter 5

1. William Norwood Brigance, *Speech: Its Techniques and Disciplines in a Free Society* (New York: Appleton-Century-Crofts, 1961), 34–35.

2. Arthur Lessac, *The Use and Training of the Human Voice: A Practical Approach to Speech and Voice Dynamics* (New York: DBS, 1967), 28–29.

3. Ibid.

4. Ibid., 30.

5. Ibid., 30–42.

6. Horace G. Rahskopf, *Basic Speech Improvement* (New York: Harper & Row, 1965), 253–54.

7. Brigance, 350–51.

8. Virgil A. Anderson, *Training the Speaking Voice* (New York: Oxford University Press, 1942), 56.

9. Anderson, 61ff.

10. Henning, 163–64.

11. Anderson, 79–80.

12. Brigance, 351.

13. Ibid.
14. Ibid., 352.
15. Anderson, 103.
16. Brigance, 352. The drawing of resonators is from p. 353 of Brigance.
17. Lessac, 17ff.
18. Ibid., 56ff. The drawing illustrating the "megaphone" shape is from Lessac, p. 18.
19. Rahskopf, 287ff.
20. Ibid., 289.
21. Wilhelmina G. Hedde and William Norwood Brigance, *American Speech*, Third Edition (Chicago: J. B. Lippincott, 1951), 128.
22. Zimmerman, 124.

Chapter 6

1. Raymond S. Ross, *Speech Communication,* 5th. ed. (Englewood Cliffs, N. J.: Prentice-Hall, 1980), 68.
2. Beebe and Beebe, 223.
3. Ibid.
4. Hesselgrave, 431.
5. John Stewart and Gary D'angelo, *Together: Communicating Interpersonally* (Reading, Mass.: Addison Wesley, 1980), 33.
6. Pearson and Nelson, 116.
7. Loretta A. Malandro and Larry Barker, *Nonverbal Communication* (Reading, Mass.: Addison Wesley, 1983), 4.
8. Pearson and Nelson, 120.
9. Henry Ward Beecher, *Yale Lectures on Preaching*, 3 vols. (New York: Fords, Howard, & Hulbert, 1892), I.32.
10. Beebe and Beebe, 228–29.
11. Spurgeon, 100–01.
12. Beebe and Beebe, 228–29.
13. Spurgeon, 98.
14. Pearson and Nelson, 120.
15. Peter Marsh, ed., *Eye to Eye: How People Interact* (Topsfield, Mass.: Salem House, 1988), 72.
16. Beebe and Beebe, 233, and Malandro and Barker, 163.
17. Beebe and Beebe, 233.
18. Ross, 82.
19. Malandro and Barker, 276.
20. Hamilton Gregory, *Public Speaking for College and Career*, Second Edition (New York: McGraw-Hill, 1990), 263.
21. Edward T. Hall, *The Hidden Dimension* (Garden City, N.Y.: Doubleday, 1966), cited in Pearson and Nelson, 121–23.
22. Ibid.
23. Ibid.
24. Stewart and D'Angelo, 37.
25. Ibid., 33.
26. Brooks, *Speech Communication*, 175.
27. Frank Tancredi, quoted by Myron Chartier, *Preaching as Communication: An Interpersonal Perspective* (Nashville: Abingdon, 1981), 79.

28. Mark L. Knapp, *Nonverbal Communication in Human Interaction* (New York: Holt, Rinehart and Winston, 1972), 147, quoted in Hesselgrave, 437.

Chapter 7

1. Vernon Latrelle Stanfield, *Favorite Sermons of John A. Broadus* (New York: Harper & Brothers Publishers, 1959), 12.

2. John A. Broadus, *A Treatise on the Preparation and Delivery of Sermons* (Philadelphia: H.B. Garner, 1883), 319.

3. Dwight E. Stevenson and Charles F. Diehl, *Reaching People from the Pulpit* (New York: Harper & Row, 1958), 49ff.

4. Broadus, 321.

5. Chartier, 29–39.

6. Haddon Robinson, *Biblical Preaching* (Grand Rapids, Mich.: Baker Book House, 1980), 179–89.

7. Broadus, 339ff.

8. Spurgeon, 134.

9. Edgar DeWitt Jones, *The Royalty of the Pulpit* (New York: Harper & Brothers, 1951), 55.

10. Broadus, 362–63.

11. Ibid., 380.

12. Brigance, 400–01. Brigance suggested a distance to noise ratio as follows, "The intensity of sound varies inversely as the square of the distance from the source." Simply stated, the hearer receives a strong vocal signal in direct proportion to how close he is to the speaker.

13. Broadus, 324.

Chapter 8

1. James Stalker, *The Preacher and His Models* (London: Hodder & Stoughton, 1891), 119.

2. Gordon Zimmerman, *Public Speaking Today* (St. Paul, Minn.: West Publishing, 1979), 116.

3. Calvin Miller, *The Empowered Communicator* (Nashville: Broadman & Holman, 1994), 193.

4. Zimmerman, 113–15.

5. Brigance, 270.

6. Stevenson and Diehl, 108.

7. Ibid.

8. Zimmerman, 112

9. M. Bautain, *The Art of Extempore Speaking*, Seventh Edition (New York: Blue Ribbon Books, 1915), 2–3.

10. Zimmerman, 117.

11. Roy W. Battenhouse, ed., *A Companion to the Study of St. Augustine* (Grand Rapids: Baker, 1979), 72–73, cited by Bill J. Leonard, "Preaching in Historical Perspective" *Handbook of Contemporary Preaching*, ed. Michael Duduit (Nashville: Broadman, 1992), 23.

12. Charles Sylvester Horne, *The Romance of Preaching* (New York: Fleming H. Revell, 1914), 58.

13. Quoted in Hans Van Der Geest, *Presence in the Pulpit,* trans. Douglas W. Stott (Atlanta: John Knox, 1981), 47.

14. Clarence E. Macartney, *Preaching without Notes* (New York: Abingdon-Cokesbury, 1946), 146.

15. Ralph Lewis, "Preaching with and without Notes," *Handbook of Contemporary Preaching,* ed., Michael Duduit (Nashville: Broadman, 1992), 411.

16. Macartney, 162–63.

17. Lewis, Ibid.

18. R. W. Dale, *Nine Lectures on Preaching* (London: Hodder & Stoughton, 1890), 151.

19. Stanfield, 12.

20. Clarence E. Macartney, *The Making of a Minister* (Great Neck, N.Y.: Channel, 1961), 129.

21. Charles Koller, *Expository Preaching without Notes* (Grand Rapids: Baker, 1962), 10, 88, 89.

22. Ralph Lewis and Greg Lewis, *Inductive Preaching* (Westchester, Ill.: Crossway, 1983), ch. 11.

23. Macartney, *Preaching without Notes,* 147.

24. Beecher, I, 71.

25. Macartney, *Preaching without Notes,* 147. Macartney names five advangates, most of which are reflected here.

26. Edwin Young, "Preaching in a Changing Culture: An interview with Michael Duduit" *Preaching,* 10:4, (1994), 6.

27. Macartney, *Preaching without Notes,* 157–58.

Chapter 9

1. See H. Grady Davis, *Design for Preaching* (Philadelphia: Fortress, 1958).

2. Eugene L. Lowry, *The Homiletical Plot* (Atlanta: John Knox, 1980).

3. David Buttrick, *Homiletic: Moves and Structures* (Philadelphia: Fortress, 1987), 23ff.

4. Donald L. Hamilton, *Homiletical Handbook* (Nashville: Broadman, 1992), 23.

5. Koller, 87.

6. Broadus, 473–74.

7. W. Y. Fullerton, *C. H. Spurgeon* (London: Williams and Norgate, 1920), 218.

8. Macartney, *Preaching without Notes,* 161.

9. Ibid.

10. Ralph L. Lewis and Greg Lewis, *Learning to Preach like Jesus* (Westchester, Ill.: Crossway, 1989).

11. See Davis.

12. Ibid., 152–53.

13. Koller, 86.

14. Davis., ch. 8.

15. See chapters 9-11 in Wayne McDill, *The Twelve Essential Skills for Great Preaching* (Nashville: Broadman & Holman, 1984) for a more detailed explanation of these functional elements of development.

16. Hesselgrave, 75–76.

17.Douglas Ehninger, Bruce E. Gronbeck, Ray E. McKerrow, and Alan H. Monroe, *Principles and Types of Speech Communication,* 10th ed. (Glenview, Ill.: Scott, Foresman and Co., 1986), 153ff.

Chapter 10

1. Charles Reynolds Brown, *The Art of Preaching* (New York: Macmillan, 1922), 155.

2. Karl Barth, *The Word of God and the Word of Man*, trans. Douglas Horton (New York: Harper & Brothers, 1957), 126.

BIBLIOGRAPHY

Anderson, Martin P., E. Ray Nichols Jr., and Herbert Booth. *The Speaker and His Audience*, 2nd ed. New York: Harper & Row, 1974.

Anderson, Virgil A. *Training the Speaking Voice*. New York: Oxford University Press, 1942.

Aristotle. *Rhetoric*. Trans. Rhys Roberts. Chicago: William Benton, 1952.

Barth, Karl. *The Word of God and the Word of Man*. Trans. Douglas Horton. New York: Harper & Brothers, 1957.

Battenhouse, Roy W.,ed. *A Companion to the Study of St. Augustine*. Grand Rapids: Baker Book House, 1979.

Bautain, M. *The Art of Extempore Speaking*. 7th ed. New York: Blue Ribbon Books, 1915.

Beebe, Steven A. and Susan J. Beebe. *Public Speaking: An Audience-centered Approach*. Inglewood Cliffs, N. J.: Prentice Hall, 1991.

Beecher, Henry Ward. *Yale Lectures on Preaching*. 3 vols. New York: Fords, Howard, & Hulbert, 1892.

Brigance, William Norwood. *Speech: Its Techniques and Disciplines in a Free Society*. New York: Appleton-Century-Crofts, 1961.

Broadus, John A. *A Treatise on the Preparation and Delivery of Sermons*. Philadelphia: H. B. Garner, 1883.

Brooks, William D. and Robert W. Heath, *Speech Communication*. Dubuque, Iowa: Wm. C. Brown Company, 1993.

Brooks, Phillips. *Lectures on Preaching*. New York: E. P. Dutton, 1898.

Buttrick, David. *Homiletic: Moves and Structures.* Philadelphia: Fortress Press, 1987.

Chartier, Myron. *Preaching as Communication: An Interpersonal Perspective.* Nashville: Abingdon Press, 1981.

Craddock, Fred B. *Preaching.* Nashville: Abingdon Press, 1985.

Dale, R. W. *Nine Lectures on Preaching.* London: Hodder & Stoughton, 1890.

Davis, H. Grady. *Design for Preaching.* Philadelphia: Fortress Press, 1958.

Ehninger, Douglas, Bruce E. Gronbeck, Ray E. McKerrow, and Alan H. Monroe, *Principles and Types of Speech Communication*, 10th ed. Glenview, Ill.: Scott, Foresman and Company, 1986.

Fant, Clyde E. *Preaching for Today.* New York: Harper & Row, 1975.

Fasol, Al. *A Complete Guide to Sermon Delivery.* Nashville: Broadman & Holman, 1996.

Fullerton, W. Y. *C. H. Spurgeon.* London: Williams and Norgate, 1920.

Gregory, Hamilton. *Public Speaking for College and Career*, 2d ed. New York: McGraw-Hill, 1990.

Hamilton, Donald L. *Homiletical Handbook.* Nashville: Broadman Press, 1992.

Hedde, Wilhelmina G. and William Norwood Brigance. *American Speech.* 3d ed. Chicago: J. B. Lippincott, 1951.

Henning, James H. *Improving Oral Communication.* New York: McGraw-Hill, 1966.

Hesselgrave, David. *Communicating Christ Cross-Culturally.* 2d ed. Grand Rapids: Zondervan Publishing House, 1991.

Hollingsworth, H. L. *The Psychology of the Audience.* New York: American Book Company, 1977.

Jacks, G. Robert. *Getting the Word Across.* Grand Rapids: William B. Eerdmans Publishing, 1995.

Jones, Edgar DeWitt. *The Royalty of the Pulpit.* New York: Harper & Brothers, 1951.

Koller, Charles W. *Expository Preaching without Notes.* Grand Rapids: Baker Book House, 1962.

Kooienga, William H. *Elements of Style for Preaching.* Grand Rapids: Zondervan Publishing House, 1989.

Leonard, Bill J. "Preaching in Historical Perspective." *Handbook of Contemporary Preaching.* Michael Duduit ed., Nashville: Broadman Press, 1992.

Lessac, Arthur. *The Use and Training of the Human Voice: A Practical Approach to Speech and Voice Dynamics.* New York: DBS Publications, 1967.

Lewis, Ralph L. with Greg Lewis. *Inductive Preaching.* Westchester, Ill.: Crossway Books, 1983.

_____. *Learning to Preach like Jesus.* Westchester, Ill.: Crossway Books, 1989.

Lewis, Ralph. "Preaching with and without Notes." *Handbook of Contemporary Preaching.* Michael Duduit ed., Nashville: Broadman Press, 1992.

Lowry, Eugene L. *The Homiletical Plot.* Atlanta: John Knox Press, 1980.

Macartney, Clarence. *Preaching without Notes.* New York: Abingdon-Cokesbury, 1946.

_____. *The Making of a Minister.* Great Neck, N.Y.: Channel, 1961.

_____. *Six Kings of the American Pulpit.* Philadelphia: Westminster Press, 1942.

Malandro, Loretta A. and Larry Barker. *Nonverbal Communication.* Reading, Mass.: Addison Wesley, 1983.

Marsh, Peter. Editor. *Eye to Eye: How People Interact.* Topsfield, Mass.: Salem House, 1988.

Matthews, Alice. "He Said, She Heard." *Leadership.* XVII:4, Fall 1995.

McDill, Wayne. *The Twelve Essential Skills for Great Preaching.* Nashville: Broadman & Holman, 1989.

Miller, Calvin. *The Empowered Communicator.* Nashville: Broadman & Holman, 1994.

Mohler, R. Albert. "A Theology of Preaching." *Handbook of Contemporary Preaching.* Nashville: Broadman Press, 1992.

Pearson, Judy Cornelia and Paul Edward Nelson. *Understanding and Sharing: An Introduction to Speech Communication.* Sixth Edition. Dubuque, Iowa: Wm. C. Brown, 1994.

Rahskopf, Horace G. *Basic Speech Improvement.* New York: Harper & Row, 1965.

Robinson, Haddon. *Biblical Preaching.* Grand Rapids, Mich.: Baker Book House, 1980.

Ross, Raymond S. *Speech Communication*, Fifth Edition. Englewood Cliffs, N.J.: Prentice-Hall, 1980.

Sack, Michael. "The Multiplex Congregation." *Leadership* XVI:4, Fall 1995.

Simpson, Matthew. *Lectures on Preaching.* New York: Phillips & Hunt, 1879.

Spurgeon, C. H. *Lectures to My Students.* Grand Rapids: Zondervan Publishing House, 1955.

Stanfield, Vernon Latrelle. *Favorite Sermons of John A. Broadus.* New York: Harper & Brothers Publishers, 1959.

Stevenson, Dwight E. and Charles F. Diehl. *Reaching People from the Pulpit.* New York: Harper & Row, 1958.

Stewart, John and Gary D'angelo. *Together: Communicating Interpersonally.* Reading, Mass.: Addison Wesley, 1980.

Stott, John R. W. *The Preacher's Portrait.* Grand Rapids: William B. Eerdmans Publishing, 1961.

Van Der Geest, Hans. *Presence in the Pulpit,* trans. Douglas W. Stott, Atlanta: John Knox Press, 1981.

Vines, Jerry. *A Guide to Effective Sermon Delivery.* Chicago: Moody Press, 1986.

Wells, Lynn K. *The Articulate Voice: An Introductipon to Voice and Diction.* 2d ed. Scottsdale, Ariz.: Gorsuch Scarisbrick, 1993.

Wiersbe, Warren W. *Living with the Giants.* Grand Rapids: Baker Book House, 1993.

Young, Edwin. "Preaching in a Changing Culture: An interview with Michael Duduit." *Preaching.* 10:4, 1994.

Zimmerman, Gordon. *Public Speaking Today.* St. Paul, Minn.: West Publishing, 1979.

INDEX

Tone Language 74

U

Understanding People 44

V

Vocal Cords 79
Vocal Tone 79
Voice Problems 79-81

W

Whitefield, George 137
Wisdom
   Discernment of 12
   Hindrances to 11

Word 8
   Definition 8
Word Language 74
Word of God 9
   Hearing of 9
Written Communication 157

Y

Young, Ed 147
Young, Kimball 40